WHAT A
FRIEND
WE HAVE IN
JESUS

WHAT A
FRIEND
WE HAVE IN
JESUS

SEVENTY
PEN PORTRAITS
OF THE MASTER
IN POETRY & PROSE

GOSPEL FOLIO PRESS
304 Killaly Street West, Port Colborne, ON L3K 6A6
Available in the UK from JOHN RITCHIE LTD.
40 Beansburn, Kilmarnock, Scotland

Published by Gospel Folio Press
304 Killaly Street West, Port Colborne, ON L3K 6A6
Web store: www.gospelfolio.com
Order phone line in North America: 1-800-952-2382

   ISBN 1-882701-92-5

Printed in the United States of America

Contents

Dedication

There would seem to be only one fitting Subject
to whose singular glory
the compilers would commit this little volume:

*Now unto Him that is able to keep you from falling,
and to present you faultless before the presence of His glory
with exceeding joy, to the only wise God our Saviour,
be glory and majesty, dominion and power,
both now and ever. Amen.*
Jude 1:24-25

The Everlasting Father is His Name.
His years fail not. No shade of change can fall
To dim His stainless luster; for when all
Decays and ages, Christ remains the same.

Yet hath He known Time's changing seasons, too.
The vernal freshness; summer's glory brief;
The fruitful autumn and the garnered sheaf;
Chill winter's icy flake—all these He knew.

So when with numb despair I turn away
From some fair blossom withering Time has slain,
I find in heaven a Heart that knows my pain;
A Heart that understands a winter's day.

He best can sympathize; He knoweth best
The texture of our being, woof and warp.
Yea, all the ten-toned strings of life's great harp,
True Son of David, echo in Thy breast.
—*James S. Tait*

At the End of Myself

Avis B. Christiansen

At the end of myself—
'Tis there, Lord, I find
The fullness of heavenly grace;
The hand that uplifts, when all others have failed,
The strength that upholds, when the foe has assailed;
The love that enfolds when the last hope has paled—
'Tis there, Lord, I see Thy blest face.

At the end of myself—
With no haven in sight,
Alone on a wild, seething sea;
'Tis there, on the billows I glimpse Thy blest form,
That stills the wild breakers and quiets the storm.
With Thee on my side I need feel no alarm,
Sweet peace is Thy portion to me.

At the end of myself—
What matters it, Lord,
If all earthly comforts should flee?
If only I find at the close of the day,
When life's futile pleasures have vanished away,
Thy smile, as before Thee my trophies I lay—
What matters if I have but Thee?

Foreword

This world, though fallen, still catches us by surprise with its beauty. Perhaps heading home after a long day, we are weary and preoccupied when suddenly the road turns toward the setting sun. There before us on God's outsized canvas is the interplay of light and shadow cast against nothing more than dust floating in space and condensing water particles. Yet this panoramic extravaganza is for one night only. Tomorrow will highlight exquisite peach and crimson or brooding blues and purples rather than the pale yellow and rich pewter in the sky tonight. In fact, each place on the planet receives a unique evening decor, not static but changing by the moment as the sunlight pirouettes across earth's canopy of blue.

When the last ray has fled from view, the encroaching darkness acts like black velvet, setting off the diamond-stars in the heavenly Jeweler's window. Worlds unknown, unmeasured, unnumbered fill the universe with the reflected glory of their Maker. If the naked eye can only see about 2,500 stars, what do the untold billions of stellar bodies tell us about the lavish generosity of our God?

Who can capture in words the blazing hues of the autumn foliage somehow painted on the leaves by the pale fingers of the frost? Or the riotous combinations of color on the fish darting through the coral reefs? See the serendipitous journey of the butterfly, feinting this way and that across the meadow or the rainbow at the end of which is something infinitely better than a pot of gold—the covenant promise of God. Can we reproduce the iridescent plumage of the wood duck or the gossamer web of the spider? Think of the massive mountain peaks sculpted in gigantic slabs of variegated stone, mantled with pine forests and wearing crowns of glistening snow. By a word here, a command there, our Friend made it all.

But surely there are more beautiful sights than this! Earth is a mere footstool to heaven's glorious throne (Isa. 66:1). Earth's vaunted gold is paving material for heaven's street. Paul the wordsmith who visited heaven, laid down his pen, confessing that earth's languages are useless to describe that glorious land (2 Cor. 12:4).

The sight of heaven will in a moment dissolve from our hearts any fondness we have had for things terrestrial. Then we will begin to understand what our Lord meant when He hinted at the relative scale of things in terms like this: *"the field is the world"* as if this planet is only a distant plot on the Landowner's vast estate. Or to use an even more dramatic figure, Hebrews 1 describes the whole universe as work clothes the Lord has put on to accomplish His purposes: *"They all shall wax old as doth a garment; and as a vesture shalt Thou fold them up, and they shall be changed: but Thou art the same, and Thy years shall not fail"* (vv. 11-12).

Yet even the sights of heaven have been far surpassed in beauty. When John describes that perfect place, he tells us of an object of such breathtaking splendor that it draws every eye in heaven away from golden street, pearly gate, crystal sea, cherub and seraph, away from thrones and diadems and every other glory there. *"And I beheld, and, lo, in the midst of the throne...stood a Lamb as it had been slain...."* (Rev. 5:6). The most eye-capturing, soul-thrilling, heart-stopping sight anyone will ever see is that Lamb who died to bear away the sin of the world.

Society is filled with distractions of every kind, designed to appeal to the ravenous appetite of the eyes (1 Jn. 2:16), an appetite never satiated (Eccl. 1:8). But God has provided an object on which, fixing the eyes of our hearts there, we will find not only ourselves transfixed but transformed. This is the divine Antidote to the human dilemma: *"But we all, with [unveiled] face beholding as in a [mirror] the glory of the Lord, are changed into the same image from glory to glory, even as by the Spirit of the Lord"* (2 Cor. 3:18).

The portraits of our Lord both in poetry and prose that are included in this volume are from the pens of men and women who discovered by personal experience what our Beloved is *"more than"* any other beloved (Song of Solomon 5:9). Their desire in writing was to share with others something of the beauties they had found in the

One who is *"altogether lovely."* They each had embraced the matchless truth contained in the line from Joseph Scriven's well-beloved hymn, *What a Friend We Have in Jesus.*

The searching for and selecting of these essays and poems was begun as the result of a personal longing by the compilers to love this Friend more, and to be more like Him. We are happy to share with you the fruit of our exploration and trust the benefit you enjoy in reading this collection will be as happy and as helpful as we found it while discovering them.

THE COMPILERS
December 2002

What a Friend We Have in Jesus

Joseph Scriven

What a Friend we have in Jesus
All our sins and griefs to bear!
What a privilege to carry
Everything to God in prayer;
O what peace we often forfeit,
O what needless pain we bear,
All because we do not carry
Everything to God in prayer!

Have we trials and temptations?
Is there trouble anywhere?
We should never be discouraged,
Take it to the Lord in prayer.
Can we find a friend so faithful
Who will all our sorrows share?
Jesus knows our every weakness—
Take it to the Lord in prayer.

Are we weak and heavy laden,
Cumbered with a load of care?
Precious Saviour, still our refuge—
Take it to the Lord in prayer.
Do thy friends despise, forsake thee?
Take it to the Lord in prayer;
In His arms He'll take and shield thee,
Thou wilt find a solace there.

The Incomparable Son

A. C. Rose

The Lord Jesus Christ dominates the Scriptures as the sun dominates our solar system. As the Eternal Son, He acts through creation and history. As the virgin's Son, He joins the stream of our race, the tributary destined to unite the currents of Jew and Gentile, and to divide our river into two courses: one flowing with ever-increasing depth to the ocean of everlasting love; the other flowing darkly, a torrent of unbelief and enmity, to be swallowed up at last in the Saharan sands of the second death.

No article, no book, no library, no university can contain the infinite treasure of the revelation of God in His Son. Indeed the world itself cannot contain the books about Him that should be written. He is the master *Theme* of prophecy; He is the *Source* of the music of the Psalms; He is the *Judge,* administering the holy, righteous law; He is the *Hero* of the Gospels; He is the *Authority* of the Acts; He is the *Subject* of the Epistles; He is the enthroned *Lamb* and glorious *Lord* of the Revelation. Alas! He is also the despised and rejected Saviour of the world; the disobeyed Head of the Church; the Perfect Guest wounded in the house of His friends; the long-absent King, who will suddenly return to take account of His servants.

To escape being overwhelmed by the exceeding riches of the grace of God, we concentrate attention on a few of the words in the Epistle to the Hebrews. With the exception of the First Epistle of John, all the other Epistles begin with a man: Paul, Peter, James, Jude. Hebrews begins with the greatest word in any language—God. But immediately associated with Him is His Son so that far from being terrified by the awe-full word, we are delighted by the assurance that the Son is the Father's Heir, demonstrating His power; the Father's radiance, expressing His character; the Father's provided sacrifice, manifesting His mercy, and the Father's Companion at the right hand of His Majesty. Then lest this high estate should be thought comparable with principalities and powers, the angelic host is revealed, ranked immeasurably far below the Son. He is the Son, they are servants; to Him alone belongs deity. He is the only begotten Son in whom dwells all the fullness of the Godhead bodily.

The writer of this Epistle, skillfully hidden from our sight in the shadow of the Holy Spirit's hand, is enamored with his subject, and as an instructed scribe, he brings forth from the Scriptures a wealth of comparison and contrast, to be woven into a wonderful revelation of his Lord. He will marshal the men and women of faith in noble array; he will pronounce the most solemn words of warning, but all will be pressed into the service of the Incomparable Son, to whom he frequently refers without title in deepest reverence as Jesus, teaching us that in that solitary word is all the grandeur belonging to the name of God.

"We see Jesus!" (2:9) he cries, after a disappointing glance at a world which fallen man has spoiled. From man—the monarch who has lost his crown—he turns to the One who, laying aside His native glory, is found in human fashion that He may become representative Man, and as a supreme act of sacrifice, taste death for His fellows and fulfill His name, "Jehovah the Saviour."

To this basic sight, the eyes of faith repeatedly return; it is the first sight of faith on earth; it will be the central sight of heaven, *"A Lamb as it had been slain."* Oh! satisfying sight; the Son of God who loved me and gave Himself for me, that He might be a merciful and faithful High Priest to make propitiation for the sins of His people.

This is He who has passed into the heavens, *"Jesus the Son of God"* (4:14), able to sympathize, having triumphed over all temptation. With such a Mediator, we are urged to hold fast our confession. With such a Man in such a place, with such evidences of His perfect love, how can we let it go? "Hold Him fast!" cried traitorous Judas to the soldiers in the Garden. "Hold Him fast!" is the burden of this Epistle to the Hebrews and to us, *"lest at any time we should slip away."* Then as a safeguard against reliance on our own resources, we read: *"We might have a strong consolation, who have fled for refuge to lay hold upon the hope set before us: which hope we have as an anchor of the soul both sure and steadfast, and which entereth into that within the veil; whither the Forerunner is for us entered, even Jesus"* (6:18-20). The feeble grasp of faith has gripped the mighty promise, which like an anchor holds beyond our sight. It is better there, for it is where He is, attached to Him inseparably. The rains descend, the floods come, the winds blow and beat upon us, but to the obedience of faith there is no overthrow, for none can pluck our hand from His, or His from ours, or either from His Father's.

To make assurance doubly sure, He has entered into a covenant of grace which is final, eternal, and satisfying because it is sealed by the blood of the Great Shepherd of the sheep. It is based equally on what God and the Man of His right hand have done. *"By so much hath Jesus become a Surety of a better covenant"* (7:22), and He in all His perfections suits our need, for He is *"holy, harmless, unde-filed, separate from sinners, and made higher than the heavens."* But more so, if we have been made partakers of this new covenant, then where Sinai failed, Calvary succeeds. The promise is fulfilled: *"I will put My laws into their minds, and write them upon their hearts, and I will be to them a God and they shall be to Me a people."*

Nor is the work of grace ended yet, since the Father's heart desires worshippers for His glory, and for the full exercise of their ransomed powers. Therefore *"boldness to enter the holiest by the blood of Jesus"* is granted (10:19). The exclusive privilege of one member of one family of one race has become the inclusive birthright of all the people of God. Each has an abiding place at the mercy-seat by virtue of that sacrifice which not only cancels guilt, but confers the privi-leges of access and affection (formerly enjoyed only by the Son) upon those of whom He says: *"Behold I and the children whom Thou has given Me.")* Then lest these blood-bought privileges should be to us only theoretical, we are urged to draw near with a true heart. How can we stay away? What attractions can rival the presence of the Father and the Son?

For a little while there is another parallel phase of experience; for although we have such a privileged place in the heavenlies, we have also responsibilities in a very different place among the shaken, overturning things of time; yet the secret of the sanctuary is the pledge of victory in every conflict. *"Looking unto Jesus, the Captain*

and Perfecter of faith" (12:2). Not short-sightedly peering towards some faint object, but gazing on One who is just ahead, who will never leave us to our own resources; who, having triumphed gloriously, is leading us on through enemies impotent to harm us while we follow obediently in His steps.

The battlefield passes from view, and we are seen on Mount Zion, walking in the city of the living God, heavenly Jerusalem, graced by an innumerable company of angels, numbered among the general assembly and Church of the Firstborn, in the presence of God our Judge and Justifier, and with Jesus the Mediator of the new covenant, and His precious blood that has made our peace (12:22–24). This is our Homeland; here we breathe our native air and speak the vernacular of our chosen clan; here we sing the psalms of victory to celebrate the Victor's fame. On Him our eyes are fastened, for He is altogether lovely; grace has been poured into His lips—they are like lilies dropping sweet-smelling myrrh; His words contain all the music of David's harp, all the wisdom of Solomon, the eloquence of Isaiah, and the pathos of Jeremiah. *"Never man so spake,"* for never man so prayed, worked, loved, suffered, died and overcame.

This is our Lord Jesus, who to bring us to His Father and our Father, suffered outside the gate (13:12). And lest the Firstborn should be separated from His brethren, He allows us to share the fellowship of His sufferings, the shame of His cross outside the camp, where His blessed footsteps are so clearly seen. So He prepares us for that moment when we shall be glorified together, and the incomparable Son of God shall see the travail of His soul and shall be satisfied.

My Beloved Friend

James G. Deck

Oh what is thy Beloved?
They oft inquire of me;
And what in my Beloved
Surpassing fair I see?
Is it the heavenly splendor
In which He shines above?
His riches, and dominions,
That won my heart's best love?

Oh no! 'tis not His glories
He's worthy of them all!
'Tis not the throne and scepter
Before which angels fall!
I view with heart exulting
Each crown His head adorns;
But, oh, He looks most lovely,
Wearing His crown of thorns.

I'm glad to see His raiment
Than snow more spotless white,
Refulgent with its brightness,
More dazzling than the light;
But more surpassing lovely
His form appears to me,
When, stripped and scourged
    and bleeding,
He hung upon the tree.

With warmest adoration
I see Him on the throne,
And join the loud hosannas
That His high virtues own;
But, oh, most blessed Jesus,
I must confess to Thee,
More than the throne of glory
I love that sacred tree.

I joy to see the diadems
Upon Thy royal brow;
The state and power and majesty
In which Thou sittest now:
But 'tis Thyself, Lord Jesus,
Makes heaven seem heaven to me,
Thyself as first I knew Thee,
Uplifted on the tree.

Though higher than the highest,
Most mighty King Thou art,
Thy grace, and not Thy greatness
First touched my rebel heart:
Thy sword, it might have
    slain me,
Thine arrows drunk my blood;
But 'twas Thy cross subdued me,
And won my heart to God.

Thy scepter rules creation,
Thy wounded hand rules me;
All bow before thy footstool,
I but the nail-prints see:
Aloud they sound Thy titles,
Thou Lord of lords most high;
One thrilling thought
    absorbs me—
This Lord for me did die!

Oh, this is my Beloved,
There's none so fair as He;
The chief among ten thousand,
He's all in all to me:
My heart it breaks with longing
To dwell with Him above,
Who wooed me first, and
    won me
By His sweet dying love.

The Coming of Christ

David Anderson-Berry

The whole world was rolling down the ages in darkness to its doom. Did the hosts of happy beings that people the regions of unsullied light peer over the battlements of heaven and mark with sadness its downward course? Did the glorious beings that flash before the face of Him who sits upon the throne shudder as from that dark world arose groans and curses, sobs and cries, ribald laughter, horrible blasphemy, shouts and yells of licensed massacre from multitudinous battlefields?

As Professor Huxley writes, "If our ears were sharp enough to hear all the cries of pain that are uttered in the earth by men and beasts, we should be deafened by one continuous scream." Any help? Any hope? None! none! for who can stay a world that has cut itself loose from its God and has bidden an eternal defiance to its Creator?

And yet, as they well might ponder over that insoluble enigma, the eternal King rises from His throne and, laying aside the scepter of the universe, the mantled splendor of deity, steps from star to star until He reaches the door of our dark world over which might truly be written, "Abandon hope, all ye that enter here."

As befits His dignity, there shines a light, unearthly in its brilliance, from the band of heaven's glorious torchbearers; there sounds a blare of trumpets from the heralds of the court of Glory, the music of the spheres made audible for once! But for some sleepy shepherds, startled from their midnight watch on the green slopes of Bethlehem's pastures, the light that had ne'er shone on hill and dale before had shined forth unobserved, the cadences that ne'er had floated over the homes and haunts of men before had sounded in vain as far as this world was concerned.

And when that door which separates this world of sense and sin from that world of spirit and glory had swung back for once in all its history *inwards*, the Lord of glory entered as a little Child swaddled in the poor linen of a toiler's home and cradled in a manger! And this was how the Lord of the universe came to the dark world He had loved and lost awhile, which He yet loved with a love stronger than death, and, loving, sought amidst the night of Time until He found it.

The scene changes. It is no longer midnight; it is now high noon. It is no longer the open courtyard of the inn of Bethlehem; it is the road that, winding down the slopes of Olivet, climbs to the great gate of the city, the Holy City—Jerusalem. It is no longer a solitary silence broken by the champing of cattle and the faint, low cry of one in pain; it is the meeting of two crowds—the one bearing in its front a young Man in the prime of life riding on a colt, the foal of an ass, and strewing the road with garments and greenery; the other pouring forth from the city's portal, lining the way, and mingling their voices in the great cry of *"Hosanna! O save!"*—the cry that once slaves, captives, subdued rebels, submissive citizens, sent up in the presence of a conqueror, thereby entreating mercy. Listen how the two crowds unite in using the words penned many centuries before by the Psalmist: *"Blessed is He that cometh in the Name of the Lord"* (Ps. 118:26). It is the acclamation of the Coming One. Time on tiptoe all down the ages had been shouting, "He is coming!"

"He is coming!" has been the testimony of prophet, priest and king. "He is on the way!" murmurs each gush of blood that flows from every sacrifice. Trumpets caught up the whisper and pealed the glad tidings forth until the listening air, learning the lesson, repeated it in each wave of sound that broke on the encircling everlasting hills.

And now the whole city is moved, for old men and children, young men and maidens, wives and virgins, vigorous youth and halting old age, are streaming forth from court and alley, from terraced slope and darksome bazaar, and meeting the multitudes from the surrounding villages and hamlets, join their voices in a mighty shout, *"Hosanna in the highest!"*

We have seen Him come to the door of the world; now we see Him come to the gate of the capital. Again, if men's ears had been trained to catch the strains of heavenly music, they would have heard the glory song, the sweet antiphon of the skies: *"Lift up your heads, O ye gates; and be ye lift up, ye everlasting doors; and the King of Glory shall come in. Who is this King of glory?...The Lord of Hosts, He is the King of glory!"* Had men's eyes been opened, they would have seen the glory Moses desired to see—the Shekinah that once flamed and glowed behind the veil in the temple that stood on yonder sacred mount; but it was hidden from their sight. And as the low thunder of the groundswell breaking on the beach, borne inland on the wings of the night wind, tells the listener of the coming storm, so the low murmur of *"Who is this?"* from the learned critics on the outskirts of the throng betokened the coming tempest. Soon from a sea of faces white with rage breaking around that central weary Figure into a spray of clenched fists there would arise that awful cry: *"Crucify Him! Crucify!"* The same crowd, the same lips, but managed by a malignant genius that knows no tiring—the passion of persecution. Is it the memory of this that enables James to pour a stream of scorching lava in the form of words over the sins of the tongue? *"Out of the same mouth proceedeth blessing and cursing."*

Thus unknown the King of glory rides on His way while the multitudes pursue their course; and the frowning portal looks down in stony silence on all this evanescent clamor of many tongues and swallows up the shouting throngs to emerge another day when He who rides the cynosure of adoring eyes then shall walk all gory to Golgotha, and they who vie in shouting *"Hosanna—O Save!"* the loudest shall cry, *"Away with Him! Away with Him!"*

And all the while He knew and suffered patiently the adulations of fickle men, for it was written, *"Rejoice greatly, O daughter of Zion; shout, O daughter of Jerusalem: behold thy King cometh unto thee"* (Zech. 9:9). I fear lest we often underrate the love and patience of Him who said, *"Lo, I come (in the volume of the Book it is written of Me) to do Thy will, O God."*

—*Pictures in Acts,* Glasgow: Pickering & Inglis, n.d.

Love's Flood Tide

William Rees (1802-1883), vv. 1, 2
Author Unknown, v. 3;
Wm. Edwards, trans. from Welsh

Here is love, vast as the ocean,
Lovingkindness as the flood,
When the Prince of Life, our Ransom,
Shed for us His precious blood.
Who His love will not remember?
Who can cease to sing His praise?
He can never be forgotten,
Throughout heaven's eternal days.

On the mount of crucifixion,
Fountains opened deep and wide;
Through the floodgates of God's mercy
Flowed a vast and gracious tide.
Grace and love, like mighty rivers,
Poured incessant from above,
And heaven's peace and perfect justice
Kissed a guilty world in love.

Let me all Thy love accepting,
Love Thee, ever all my days;
Let me seek Thy kingdom only
And my life be to Thy praise;
Thou alone shalt be my glory,
Nothing in the world I see.
Thou hast cleansed and sanctified me,
Thou Thyself hast set me free.

The Compassion of Christ

D. L. Moody

S ome time ago, I began to read the Bible carefully to study Bible characters. I read through the four Gospels, and my heart was moved. When I look over an audience and think of the wretchedness and misery that you and I do not see, that He does see, I think I can understand what this means: *"When He saw the multitude, He was moved with compassion."* His heart went out to them.

We ought to have more compassion for the unfortunate, the erring, and the fallen. How many times I have had to upbraid myself for this. I believe it would be a very easy thing to reach the unfortunate and distressed if we had the spirit of the good Samaritan.

People say, "I wish I had it." How can we get it? Listen. Suppose a great misfortune has overtaken you; wouldn't you like to have someone come right along and help you? Wouldn't you? I believe there is not a man or woman, I don't care how rich or poor they may be, who does not need at some hour in their lives a little human sympathy, a little ministration of love, or helpful words from somebody else. Each heart has its own bitterness, each one has his own trouble and sorrow. We are too apt to think that others do not need or care for our compassion.

Now if you want to get the spirit of compassion, just think of someone among your acquaintance who is in trouble—someone who is in distress, or who has had some great misfortune. And who has not? Then imagine that their trouble is yours.

I used to spend my summers in Chicago; probably fifteen-hundred to two thousand children were in our Sunday school and very few of them had a church home. When sickness or death came into their families they used to send for me. I sometimes attended three or four funerals a day. I could go to a funeral and see a mother walk up to the coffin of her loved one, and hear sobs and wails of anguish that were enough to break a heart of stone, but I heard them so often they wouldn't move my heart. I had become hardened.

One day my wife told me that one of the children in my Sunday school had been drowned. I took my little girl, four years old, and started for the home of the child. Some working men and women had dragged the little one's body from the water, and the mother sat by the dead child, stroking her hair, as the water was dripping down upon the floor. It was her firstborn child. Little Adelaide used to go to the Chicago River and gather floating wood for the fire. That day she had gone as usual; she saw a piece of wood a little way from the bank and, in stretching out her hand to reach it, she slipped and fell into the water and was drowned.

There were four children in the room. The husband sat in the corner—drunk. The mother said between her sobs and tears: "You see the condition my husband is in. I have had to take in washing to get a living for my children, and I have had to care for him. He has never provided for us, or done a day's hard work in five years. Adelaide was my companion. I have no money to buy a shroud or coffin for her. Oh, I wish you could help me."

I laid down the money for the coffin and the shroud. Then she said, as the tears rolled down her face, "Can you help me find a place to bury her?"

"Yes," I said, "I will attend to that."

I made a memorandum of what was wanted, and I did it all very mechanically. Then I took my little child by the hand and started out. When we reached the street, my little girl said, "Papa, suppose we were very poor, and Mamma had to wash for a living; and I had to go to the river to get sticks to make a fire. If I should see a big stick and should try to get it and should fall into the water and get drowned, would you feel bad?"

"Feel bad! Why, my child, I do not know what I should do. You are my only daughter, and if you were taken from me I think it would break my heart," and I took her to my bosom and kissed her.

"Papa," she said, "did you feel bad for that poor mother?" The child had been shocked at her own father. How that question cut me to the heart. I could not speak.

I led the child home, then I went into my room and turned the key to the door. I walked up and down the room all that day. I said to myself: "You profess to be a disciple of Jesus Christ, and to represent Him, and you went to that heart-broken woman, and you left her there with a drunken husband." I got on my knees and asked God to forgive me, and to give me a tender heart, that if I ever saw people in trouble I might sympathize with them.

I went back to that poor woman's house, and read the fourteenth chapter of John, and I told the mother where Adelaide had gone, and prayed that the Lord might heal the mother's wounded heart. We fastened the lid of the coffin, got a carriage, and put the poor mother and her four little children into it. Last of all, little Adelaide's coffin was put into the carriage with them. The husband was still drunk and did not realize what was going on.

The cemetery was seven miles away. I had not been there for many years. I thought my time was too precious to go there. I said, "I can't let that mother go alone and bury her child," and rode the seven miles and comforted her all I could. I could weep with her then. "Suppose it was my child!" was the thought that kept coming into my mind.

We buried Adelaide in the Potter's Field. We had no sooner lowered her body into the grave than we were ordered off the place. As the mother tore herself away, she turned and looked towards the little grave and moaned: "I haven't always been able to pay my rent, and have lived among strangers all my life. I have always thought that was hard, and oh, it is hard! But it is harder to bury my Adelaide here, to leave her here in an unmarked grave in the Potter's Field. I am afraid I shall not know where she is laid."

I thought it would be very hard for me to lay my little girl in a pauper's grave. I said to myself, "I will never bury a child in a pauper's grave again as long as I live."

On the next Sunday I told the story before my Sunday school, and, although they were all poor children, we raised money and bought a lot of our own in which a hundred children could be buried. Before I could get the deed, another heart-broken mother came and said: "Mr. Moody, my little girl died today. Can I bury her in that lot?"

She asked me if I would go to the funeral, and say a few words,

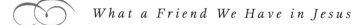

and bury her. I said I would. I well remember the first burial in that lot. The little grave was dug under an oak tree.

When we came to lay the child in it, I asked the mother: "What was the name of your little girl?"

"Emma," she said.

That was the name of my own little girl, my only daughter. Do you think I could not grieve, that I could not weep and sympathize?

In a little while, another mother came. Her little boy had died, and she wanted to bury him in that lot. We made a grave close to Emma's grave. After making a few remarks, I turned to the mother and said, "What was the name of your boy?"

"Willie," she said.

That was the name of my only boy at that time. So strange that the first two little bodies let down into those graves should bear the names of my two dear ones. Do you think I could not weep with that mother, that I did not have compassion, and that my heart did not ache for her?

Soon after, I went to Europe. I was gone a year and a half, and when I returned to Chicago, one of the first things I did was go to that cemetery. The lot was filled with little graves. I have often said that I should like to be buried there with those little ones, and when my Master comes, and they rise to meet Him, I should like to go up with them.

Have you got compassion yourself? Don't you think there's need of it? Ought we not to cultivate it? Oh, my friends, what conception can you form of the compassion of Jesus? He knows what human nature is. He knows what poor, weak, frail mortals we are, and how prone we are to sin. He will have compassion upon you; He will reach out His tender hand and touch you as He did the poor leper. You will know the touch of His loving hand, for there is virtue and sympathy in it. *"He will have compassion upon us; He will subdue our iniquities; and Thou wilt cast all their sins into the depths of the sea"* (Micah 7:19).

Our Best Friend

John Newton

One there is above all others,
Well deserves the name of friend;
His is love beyond a brother's,
Costly, free, and knows no end:
They who once His kindness prove,
Find it everlasting love!

Which, of all our friends, to save us,
Would consent to shed His blood?
But our Jesus died to have us
Reconciled in Him to God:
This was boundless love indeed!
Jesus is a friend in need.

When He lived on earth abased,
Friend of sinner was His name;
Now above all glory raised
He rejoices in the same:
Still he calls them brethren, friends,
And to all their wants attends.

Could we bear for one another,
What He daily bears for us?
Yet this glorious friend and brother
Loves us, tho' we treat Him thus:
Tho' for good we render ill,
He accounts us brethren still.

O, for grace our hearts to soften!
Teach us, Lord, at length, to love;
We, alas! forget too often,
What a friend we have above;
But when home our souls are brought,
We shall love thee as we ought.

The Changelessness of Christ

William A. Gray

Consider Jesus Christ, you who have tasted and seen that He is gracious, and let your own lives testify to the fact. *"Jesus Christ the same yesterday, and to day, and for ever"* (Heb. 13:8). Think of the *"yesterday"* of any period in your own past. That *"yesterday"* had its particular needs to be supplied, its own sorrows to be soothed, its own temptations to be conquered, its own sins to be forgiven. As a memory you possess it still—a record at once both of personal unworthiness and of the faithfulness and friendship of the One who helped and sustained you through it all. But as an opportunity and a fact, *"yesterday"* has vanished. It has vanished with its needs and its circumstances, and *"today"* comes with needs and circumstances of its own. There are new dangers to be faced, new duties to be done, new griefs to be borne, and there is new guilt to be pardoned. But the Jesus Christ of *"yesterday"* is the Jesus Christ of *"today"* in all the same nearness to protect, the same strength to support, the same grace to forgive.

As *"today"* joins hands with *"yesterday"* in attesting the faithfulness of the living Christ, so "forever" will join hands with *"today."* There will be sorrows and perils ahead of us, just as there are sorrows and perils behind. And in the thought of an unknown future—with the possibilities and fears that loom large, the heart may be *"careful and troubled about many things"* (Lk. 10:41). "We have not gone this way before" is the thought that solemnizes us as we look over the boundary line separating the known *"today"* from the unknown tomorrow. But though the path is veiled and unknown, the Companion is tried and familiar. We *"know whom [we] have believed, and [are] persuaded that He is able to keep that which [we] have committed unto Him against that day"* (2 Tim. 1:12).

"What is that to thee?" He seems to say to us still, as the heart's forebodings shape themselves into many curious and anxious questions. *"Follow thou Me"* (Jn. 21:22). Experiences and circumstances may vary. They are not now in the present what they were in the past. They will not be in the future just what they are at the present. But Jesus Christ is the same. His ear as open to hear; His arm as strong to support; His wisdom as sure to guide—*"today"* as *"yesterday,"* and *"forever"* as *"today."*

It is not only our own experience that attests to this truth; we are surrounded by *"so great a cloud of witnesses"* to the dependability of this unchanging Friend as well. And since we are, let us look to Jesus, the author and finisher of *our* faith even as He was author and finisher of *theirs.* Up with those hearts from the changing to the changeless; from the passing and the dying here to the eternally living and abiding One there; from the tossing and the tumult of the waves around us to the thought of the steadfast Rock of Ages and the anchor that remains unmoved beyond the veil.

Sorrow, parting, and death may separate *"today"* from *"yesterday"*; they may separate *"tomorrow"* from *"today"*; but nothing can *"separate us from the love of God, which is in Christ Jesus our Lord"* (Rom. 8:39). So shall we secure for ourselves, amidst this restless world—and often in our own restless hearts—some inflowing from the supreme and eternal calm. So shall we remember how the life of the only wise God and our Saviour broods over our stormy and changeful histories, as the deep, untroubled sky stretches blue and still above the region of driving clouds and warring winds. For the person who remembers that his *"life is hid with Christ in God"* (Col. 3:3) there can remain an inward tranquility. Is it not His own sure promise? *"These things I have spoken unto you, that in Me ye might have peace. In the world ye shall have tribulation: but be of good cheer; I have overcome the world"* (Jn. 16:33). Then *"Return unto thy rest, O my soul"* (Ps. 116:7).

—*The Shadow of the Hand and Other Sermons,* Edinburgh: Oliphant, Anderson & Ferrier, 1885

My Beloved

John Quarles (1624-1665), adapted

Whate'er may change, in Him no change is seen,
A glorious Sun, that wanes not, nor declines;
Above the clouds and storms He walks serene,
And on His people's inward darkness shines.
All may depart—I fret not nor repine,
While I my Saviour's am, while He is mine.

While here, alas! I know but half His love,
But half discern Him, and but half adore;
But when I meet Him in the realms above,
I hope to love Him better, praise Him more,
And feel, and tell, amid the choir divine,
How fully I am His, and He is mine.

The Name Above Every Name

T. H. Darlow

A new movement in the world always has to frame new words and phrases in which to express itself. This law of human nature is operative today. Physical inventions and discoveries have created a host of strange terms to correspond. We were compelled to coin fresh words which our ancestors never heard of, before we could discourse about automobiles and submarines and airplanes. For new wine demands new bottles; and whenever the vintage ripens and the winepress fills, the bottles are not lacking.

The same thing occurs, still more conspicuously, in times of revival. Pentecost has this sure sign and sequel, that men began to speak with new tongues, as the Spirit gave them utterance. They employ old phrases in a fresh sense, they take common words and put them to nobler uses and transfigure them with holier meaning....

As soon as Christian faith spread abroad and rooted itself in heathen soil, its genius borrowed and adapted the language of its new home. The early Gentile converts did what the converts in our modern mission fields are constantly doing. They converted secular words to Christian uses....

This may be illustrated by two examples of the use of words not, in a technical sense, theological. In the Acts of the Apostles we find that the earliest Christians often spoke of their faith simply as *"the Way."* Our Lord had set them an example when He said, *"Narrow is the Way."* He Himself was a new and living Way. And so we read of the Way of God, the Way of truth, the Way of salvation, until this term becomes a kind of synonym for Christianity. The Pharisee Saul's commission said that if he found *"any of the Way"* he should bring them bound to Jerusalem, and in after years he confessed, *"I persecuted this Way unto the death"*....

Yet another and more striking example of primitive Christian dialect appears in the habit which the early Christian disciples acquired of referring to *"the Name"* as though that word stood for the Lord Jesus Christ Himself. The New Testament commonly designates our Lord either as Jesus, the Saviour, or as Christ, the Sent of God. After the resurrection these were often combined into one appellation.

But again and again we read how they preached concerning the Name. They were forbidden to speak to any man in this Name. Yet speak they must, for *"there is none other name under heaven given among men whereby we must be saved"* (Acts 4:12). Many believed on His Name and had life through His Name and were baptized in His Name. They gathered together for worship in His Name, and therefore with His Presence among them. When they offered a prayer, or gave a cup of cold water, or received a little child, it was in the Lord's Name. Whatsoever they did, in word or deed, they did all in the Name of the Lord Jesus. To name that Name was to depart from iniquity.

This characteristic formula of the early Church was more than an accident. Some, indeed, would ascribe it to the influence of ancient magic, which held that a god or demon was present whenever his name was duly uttered in an invocation. But no student of Scripture can fail to recognize in this primitive Christian usage the imitation of a far earlier Jewish habit of speech.

In the Old Testament the Name of the Lord is mentioned almost as often as the Lord Himself. For an overpowering reverence had gathered round the sacred Hebrew name of Almighty God. The Jews came to treat it as a mystery, too awful to be spoken aloud. It was so high above every name that the rabbis shrank from pronouncing its syllables. They substituted a feebler word in its place. In ordinary Jewish speech *"the Name"* came to be used as an equivalent for Jehovah.

Thus it was not by accident that the Christians fell into the custom of treating the Name of Jesus the Messiah in the same fashion as their fathers had treated the ineffable, unutterable Name of Jehovah. It bears witness to the way in which those early disciples instinctively thought of Him. For them, His Name is above every name because they beheld heaven opened and Jesus in the midst of the throne of God....

All generations of believers have proven its strange, unearthly attraction, its enduring permanence, its mighty and miraculous power. For such disciples as these, their faith is expressed in the Name of Jesus Christ, their love is centered upon Him. In every age there are multitudes of simple-hearted folk, the aged and little children, the humble and heavy-laden and the poor, to whom science is dumb and nature is dark and criticism is foolishness, who find in the Lord Jesus Himself all and more than all they need.

Not in empty words do such Christians testify to the sufficiency of their Saviour and the supremacy of His Name. They tell us that He is far better than even His own promises. They declare that they know Him as they cannot know their dearest earthly friends. In Him all the longings of the soul find their fruition, all losses have their compensation, all the ills and griefs of life have their cure.

To the worshippers of Jesus Christ His Name is far above every name that is named in this world or in that which is to come because His Life is above every life, and His Love above every love, and His Passion above every passion. Behold, and see if there be any sorrow like unto His Sorrow. His Sacrifice is above every sacrifice, His Victory above every victory. Therefore *"at the name of Jesus every knee should bow...and...every tongue should confess that Jesus Christ is Lord, to the glory of God the Father"* (Phil. 2:10-11).

—*Via Sacra,* London: Hodder and Stoughton, n.d., pp. 261-268

My Treasure

Philip Doddridge

Jesus! I love Thy charming name;
'Tis music to my ear:
Fain would I sound it out so loud
That heaven and earth should hear!

Yes, Thou art precious to my soul,
My transport, and my trust:
Jewels to Thee are gaudy toys,
And gold is sordid dust.

All my capacious powers can wish
In Thee most richly meet:
Nor to my eyes is life so dear,
Nor friendship half so sweet.

I'll speak the honors of Thy name
With my last laboring breath:
Then speechless clasp Thee in my arms—
The antidote of death.

Beholding Him

F. B. Meyer

We may enjoy the perpetual recognition of the presence of Christ. *"The world seeth Me no more; but ye see Me"* (Jn. 14:19). Nothing makes men so humble and yet so strong as the vision of Christ.

It Induces Humility

When Isaiah beheld His glory more resplendent than the sheen of the sapphire throne, he cried that he was undone. When Peter caught the first flash of His miraculous power gleaming across the waves of Galilee, just when the fish were struggling in the full net, he besought Him to depart, because he felt himself a sinful man. And when John saw Him on the Isle of Patmos, he fell at His feet as dead—though, surely, if any of the apostles could have faced Him unabashed, it had been he.

This is especially noticeable in the Book of Job. Few books are so misunderstood. It is supposed to contain the description of the victory of Job's patience; in reality it delineates its testing and failure. It shows how he who was perfect according to the measure of his light, broke down in the fiery ordeal to which he was exposed, and finally was forced to cry, *"I have heard of Thee by the hearing of the ear, but now mine eye seeth Thee; wherefore I abhor myself, and repent in dust and ashes."*

Would you be humble? Then ask the Spirit to reveal Jesus in all His matchless beauty and holiness, eliciting the confession that you are the least of saints and the chief of sinners. This is no forced estimate when we take into account the opportunities we have missed, the gifts we have misused, the time we have wasted, the light we have resisted, and the love we have not requited.

It PRODUCES STRENGTH

See that man of God prone on the floor of his chamber, shedding bitter tears of godly sorrow, not forgiving himself, though he knows himself forgiven; bowing his head as a bulrush, crying that he is helpless, broken, and at the end of himself. Will he be able to stand as a rock against the beat of temptation and the assault of the foe? Yes, for the same presence which is to him a source of humility in private will inspire to great deeds of faith and heroism when he is called to stand in the breach.

It is this vision of the present Lord that, in every age of the Church, has made sufferers strong. *"The Lord is on my right hand, I shall not be moved,"* said one. *"The Lord stood by me, and strengthened me,"* said another. In many a dark day of suffering and persecution, in the catacombs, in the dens and caves where the Waldenses hid, on the hillsides where the Covenanters met to pray, in the beleaguered cities of the Netherlands, in prison and at the stake—God's saints have looked to Him, and been lightened, and their faces have not been ashamed. *"Behold,"* said the first Christian martyr, *"I see the heavens opened, and the Son of Man standing on the right hand of God."*

O for more of the open vision of Jesus, ministered to us by the gracious Spirit! Would that His words, *"Ye behold Me,"* were more often verified in our experience! He is always with us; and if only our eyes were not holden, we should behold Him with the quick perception of the heart. Indeed, the race can only be rightly run by those who have learned the blessed secret of looking off unto Him. *"We see Jesus."*

It is a most salutary habit to say often, when one is alone, *"Thou art near, O Lord"*; *"Behold, the Lord is in this place."* We may not at first realize the truth of what we are saying. His presence may be veiled, as the forms of mountains swathed in morning cloud. But as we persist in our quest, putting away from us all that would grieve Him and cultivating the attitude of pure devotion, we shall become aware of a divine presence which shall be more to us than a voice speaking from out the Infinite.

Precious Things in Him

C. A. Coates (1862-1945)

The Light of glory shineth
At God's right hand above,
His righteousness and mercy,
The sunshine of His love.

For Jesus now is crownéd
In holy splendor there,
And God is seen effulgent
In Him so bright and fair.

The joy of grace is filling
With music all that land,
Where grace, enthroned in Jesus,
Now reigns at God's right hand.

For every thought of favor
Set forth in Christ the Son,
Delights the hosts in glory,
Their mind with God is one.

The Peace of Heaven is constant,
No voice is heard of strife;
Nor care, nor fear can ruffle
Its calm, with blessing rife.

The peace of God there reigneth
In undisputed sway,
Flows like a tranquil river
Its restful, endless day.

The Love of God pervadeth
With life and bliss supreme,
And warmth of deep affection,
That holy, happy scene.

There all is of the Father,
The outcome of His love;
Wrought by His Son and Spirit
Are all the "things above."

On things so true, so holy,
Our minds be ever set,
In search of Wisdom's treasures,
Unknown on earth as yet.

For quickly comes the moment,
When all these precious things
Shall fill the earth with gladness,
And Christ be King of kings.

Christ is All

Hy. Pickering

The central theme of the Colossian epistle is found in chapter 3:11: *"Where there is neither Greek nor Jew, circumcision nor uncircumcision, Barbarian, Scythian, bond nor free: but Christ is all, and in all."* The apostle seems to sweep aside everyone to magnify Christ. The world's greatest language—Greek; the only divine religion that ever was—Jew; religious ordinances, such as circumcision; non-religious Gentiles and races—the uncircumcised; Barbarians, or the worst kind of barbarian—Scythian; slaves who are fettered or masters who are free: all must give place to Christ, for Christ in all things *"must have the pre-eminence."*

In an epistle in which a great statement like this climaxes, we look for stages or indications of the theme going before. Notice five:

CHRIST ALL IN CREATION: *"For by Him were all things created, that are in heaven, and that are in earth, visible and invisible, whether they be thrones, or dominions, or principalities, or powers: all things were created by Him, and for Him"* (1:16). Not often in Scripture is there a repetition in the same verse: *"In Him all things were created...all things were created through Him and for Him."* Here we have the sphere, the agent, and the purpose of creation.

However men may seek to evade the fact, and modernists or evolutionists try to explain it away, this is plain. The Scriptures declare that everything in heaven and earth, everything visible and invisible, all temporal and spiritual forces and powers, were created by Christ.

The doctrines of grace, the discoveries of science, the development of history, and the divine revelation as to creation will yet harmonize in the realization that Christ is the cause, head, and goal of the created universe. *"For by Him were all things created...."*

CHRIST ALL IN CONTROL: *"And He is before all things, and by Him*

39

all things consist," or are controlled, upheld, and kept in being (1:17). John the Baptist was born six months before Jesus, yet John could say, *"He was before me"* (Jn. 1:15). Abraham lived some 2200 years before the birth of Jesus, yet Christ said, *"before Abram was, I AM."* Not "I was," but *"I AM"* (Jn. 8:58). The world was created at least 4,000 years before Christ was born in Bethlehem, yet He spoke of His being with God, *"before the world was"* (Jn. 17:5). In fact, of Him the Spirit says, *"From everlasting to everlasting Thou art God"* (Ps. 90:2), and to Him the ancient prophecy ascribes the marvelous "before all" title of *"The Father of Eternity"* (Isa. 9:6, RV, margin).

He is the Uncreated Creator of all things. *"By Him all things consist."* The vast universe of God is all kept in place, controlled, and guided by the One whom they *"slew and hanged on a tree"* (Acts 5:30). Marvelous mystery! While aged Simeon upheld Him, He upheld Simeon, and the ground on which Simeon was standing!

Sweeping from the immensity of His power to the individuality of His care and love, I remember that *"not a sparrow"* on the lonely moor or sandy desert, unknown to and unnoticed by man, falls to the ground without His knowledge (Mt. 10:29). We can come to the smallest of particles, rejoicing that \while "worlds on worlds are hanging on His hand," He cares\ for every atom of every one of His own. *"The very hairs of your head are all numbered"* (Lk. 12:7). Christ All for my all.

CHRIST ALL IN SALVATION: *"Having made peace through the blood of His cross, by Him to reconcile all things unto Himself"* (1:20). In Philippians 2:10, where His dominion is in question, it is things in heaven, earth, and hell. In Colossians 1:20, where the theme is redemption, it is only heaven and earth. Solemn thought, there is no *"blood,"* and therefore no redemption in hell. The one glad opportunity is *"now"* (2 Cor. 6:2).

Whatever else the Scripture makes plain, it makes this plain, that salvation is only by sacrifice, and that the sacrifice of an unblemished victim. The only perfect Sacrifice ever offered was the Son of God who *"made peace through the blood of His cross,"* for only once did perfect blood stain this sin-cursed earth, and that when *"the blood of His own"* (Acts 20:28, New Trans.) flowed from the Sacrifice and Victor of Calvary. *"Neither is there salvation in any other"* for Christ is alone the Author and Finisher of salvation.

CHRIST ALL IN THE CHURCH: *"...the Head, from which all the body by joints and bands...increaseth with the increase of God"* (2:19). *"And He is the Head of the Body, the Church"* (1:18).

Christ loved the Church, died for the Church, nourishes and cherishes the Church, and will yet present the Church faultless in glory. He is the Theme of worship, the Center of gathering, the Subject of ministry, the Power for service, the Object of praise in time, and of endless and ceaseless glory and triumph in eternity of every member of the Church.

Christ as Head of the Church implies three great principles: life, unity, and rule. He is the Source of spiritual life, the center of all spiritual unity, and the Sovereign of all saints. *"One is your Master, even Christ, and all ye are brethren"* (Mt. 23:8). How solemn to acknowledge as "Head of our Church" a mere human being of any description, or have any center but the God-given One.

CHRIST IS ALL IN EVERYDAY LIFE: Lest any should think that *"Christ is all"* is creational, theological, and yet not intensely practical, there is one more major theme. *"And whatsoever ye do in word or deed, do all in the Name of the Lord Jesus"* (3:17). *"Christ all"* is now linked with every thought, word, and deed, with every attitude and relationship of life. Observe how this great fact is linked with wives submiting to their husbands (v. 18), husbands loving their wives (v. 19), children obeying their parents (v. 20). As well, Paul writes: *"Fathers, provoke not your children"* (v. 21) lest they *"be discouraged;"* sympathize with and make companions of your children so that *"Christ may be all"* to parent and child alike. Mothers are not named. Was it because He who said, *"Son, behold Thy mother,"* truly knew a mother's heart; mother love needed little exhortation.

Paul then brings in servants and masters. A servant's place, however menial, is a post of honor in which he or she may glorify God, *"for ye serve the Lord Christ"* (v. 24). So too, the model master is the one who gives *"just and equal,"* knowing that he has *"also a Master in heaven."*

Thus it will be evident that in God's universe, in Christ's Church, and in the Christian family, He has the pre-eminence.

Let This Mind be in You

E. L. Bevir (1847-1922)

Son of God, from high descending,
To this lowly planet bending,
Perfect Man's undying worth,
Midst the mortal sons of earth;
Lord of all, yet seeketh He
Rude laborious poverty;
Carpenter of Nazareth,
Bowing down to stoop to death.

Heroes fall 'mid battle's thunder
Round the martyr's pyre we wonder,
But the Saviour, stooping still,
Lowest of the low must fill;
Welcomes reputation's loss
On a malefactor's cross,
There to deepest shame come down,
Foul reproach with thorny crown!

Jesus, Lord! whene'er high-minded,
Impious pride our hearts hath blinded,
Lead us back in true contrition
By Thine own sublime tuition;
May our path be e'er descending,
To Thy lowly yoke still bending,
Till with Thee in that blest hour,
Lift we up the head in power.

Heaven's Certainty

F. E. Marsh

"Certainties are remedies," says the poet. How true are his words. The businessman, when he has the certain knowledge that his business is sound and healthy, finds in the knowledge a remedy which kills his anxiety. The mariner who is guided by his chart and compass knows where the dangerous places are, and therefore has no fear of running on the rocks in his voyage, for he knows the course to steer. His certainty is the remedy against all fear. The same is true with regard to the child of God, for concerning the sure and certain hope of Christ's glad return, and the heaven of His glory, He has said, *"If it were not so, I would have told you"* (Jn. 14:2). Or, as Godet translates it, *"If our separation were to be eternal, I would have forewarned you."* Therefore heaven is sure to the believer because the promise is sure and the word given is valid.

Broadly speaking, there are four things which make the words of Christ in this setting a sure comfort.

CHRIST'S PRECIOUS DEATH OBTAINS IT. Joshua's word can open a way to the cities of earth, to the good land of milk and honey. But only the Son of God can open to the children of earth made of clay, and sons of death, the dwellings of life and heaven. And He can only do it by His death.

Christ intimates this in speaking of Himself as the Way to the Father and the gloryland, in the preposition He uses. The meaning of the word translated *"by"* in John 14:6 is "by means of." There are three other places in the Gospel of John where the word *dia* occurs. In John 3:17 it is given *"through"*; in 6:57, *"by"*; and in 10:9, *"by."* In each case, Christ's mediatorial death is stated or suggested. Because He has passed through the dark tunnel of death for sin, He can now bring us into the light of heaven's beauty and bliss. We look back on the empty Cross and it reminds us of the accepted Sacrifice; we look up to heaven's throne and behold the Christ, bearing in His body the marks of His toil and triumph.

CHRIST'S PRIESTLY PRESENCE SUSTAINS IT. Christ as our Forerunner has taken possession for us. He has already announced our coming. As John the Baptist was the forerunner of Christ and heralded forth His coming, so Christ is our Forerunner who announces our approach. The fact of Christ being in heaven not only makes it certain for us, for He is the Anchor which holds our ship (Heb. 6:19), but He also makes it attractive to us.

He is the Light of heaven, for He illuminates it (Rev. 21:23). He is the Life in the midst of it (Rev. 22:2). He is the Sustainer of heaven, for He feeds with hidden manna (Rev. 2:17). He is the Refresher of heaven, for He satisfies with the Water of Life (Rev. 21:6). He is the Center of heaven, for He is on the throne (Rev. 3:21). He is the Glory of heaven, for His Name is on every forehead; thus no one can look at another without seeing Him (Rev. 22:4). He is the Joy of heaven's constant service, for His servants serve Him (Rev. 7:15).

CHRIST'S SURE, VALID PROMISE CONTAINS IT. We cannot fathom the meaning of those words of cheer: *"If it were not so, I would have told you."* If David could cheer on his men to take Jerusalem from the Jebusites, with the assurance that there he would dwell, and they should have abodes with him, how much more should we be comforted by our Lord's words. His words of assurance give comfort to our hearts and joy to our spirits.

"What do you do without a mother to tell all your troubles to?" asked a child who had a mother to another child who had none.

"I go to Jesus," answered the little orphan. "He was mother's Friend, and He's mine, too."

"Jesus Christ is in the sky. He's away off, and has so many things to look after in heaven."

"I don't know anything about that," said the child; "all I know is, He says He will hear us—and He does."

Yes, it is enough to faith. His Word is like a rock for stability, none can move it; it is like a check for reliability, and He will surely honor it; it is like a banqueting table for accessibility, and none need leave it hungry.

CHRIST'S COMING "PAROUSIA" WILL ATTAIN IT. There is a pathos-filled incident in the life of Hugh Miller. He tells how, after his father had left home in his ship, he used to go and watch for his return. His own words tell the story best:

> I used to climb, day after day, a grassy protuberance behind my mother's house, which commands a wide reach of the Moray Firth. I would look wistfully out, long after everyone else had ceased to hope, for the sloop with the two stripes of white, and the two square topsails I never saw.

What a ring of disappointment, and a note almost of despair is heard in the words: "…I never saw!" Such disappointment can never be the believer's lot, for one glad day "the heavens shall glow with splendor," the trumpet-voice of the Archangel shall awake the dead, and the gathering shout of the Lord shall summon the living. Then together we shall be caught up to meet the Lord in the air, and be forever in His presence.

Such certainty will change our lives. We will have no difficulty living for the right world, or serving with the right motive, or having our hearts set on the right objective, if we have heaven in our eyes.

Why?

E. M. Govan

You ask me why I see no charm nor glory
In this world's pleasures, or its wealth and fame?
And why I love that Galilean story
Of One who died upon a cross of shame?
It is because my soul hath known its sinning,
The grief and darkness of that cry undone,
And at that cross has found a new beginning,
Life through the death of that dear dying One.

You ask me why I find no rest or gladness
In paths where selfish ease would while my hours?
And why I toil where hearts in bitter sadness
Lie crushed beneath sin's fierce o'erwhelming powers?
It is because I know life's thread is slender,
But one short hour, one little stretch of road,
Then yearns my heart with love divinely tender,
To seek the lost and bring them home to God.

You ask me why, what gifts I have, what graces,
Are poured an offering at His holy feet,
And why I brave the cold contemptuous faces
Of those who love this world and find it sweet;
It is because I see a distant morning
When stand God's sons around His jasper throne;
I see bright crowns those holy brows adorning,
And I, too, long to hear my Lord's *"Well done."*

Is the Lord a Wilderness to You?

Robert Lee

I n the first of Jehovah's messages through Jeremiah, the tender-hearted prophet, and recorded in Jeremiah 2, there are a number of touching questions: "What is wrong in Me?" (v. 5); "Why not inquire of Me?" (v. 6); "The priests ignore Me, why?" (v. 8); "Is there any nation so whimsical as you?" (v. 11); "Why do you act as a spoiled servant?" (v. 14); "Why have you forsaken Me?" (v. 17); "Why do you hanker after Egypt?" (v. 18), etc. The whole of the message is a series of challenging and searching queries. But surely none are so pointed and full of meaning as *"Have I become a wilderness unto Israel?"* (v. 31). The Lord a wilderness to His redeemed ones?

Repeatedly we find in the sacred records that graphic phrase, *"all that great and terrible wilderness"* (*e.g.*, Deut. 1:19), by which an attempt was made to describe the dreary places Israel had to traverse in their desert journeys. A wilderness is an undesirable place where no one cares to be. Is it not tragic to find suggested here the possibility of the Desire of Nations, the Altogether Lovely One, the Chiefest among Ten Thousand, becoming unattractive and undesired? Yet such is the inference.

One of the surest and safest proofs of a growth in grace is an ever-increasing appreciation of the finished work and the glories and beauties of the Lord. Trusting in the Lord should speedily lead to *"Delight thyself also in the Lord"* (Ps. 37:4). What a suggestive order is to be noticed there. *"Trust"* then *"do good"*; not *"do good"* and then *"trust."* No, faith first; then works. But be sure to *"do good"* after trusting. *"Trust in the Lord, and feed on His faithfulness"* (RV). That is important. As I ponder and nourish my soul on the faithfulness of God, I soon, very soon, will begin to *"delight*

[my]*self also in the Lord."* That means goodbye to the wilderness view of Christ. The wilderness becomes a garden of delights.

The saddest fact of all is that He had become as a wilderness to many of His redeemed ones. Israel stood in that relationship. Not only had they in Egypt passed under the blood for safety, but through the Red Sea for deliverance. He had given them the land flowing with milk and honey for an inheritance. What more could He have done? Though punctilious in the performance of their religious duties, they had become empty formalists, missing and losing the Lord even in His own sanctuary.

Neglect is the parent of desert lives. Only too well do we know that the less we pray, the less inclined we become to pray; the less we read the Bible, the less we desire it; and the more we neglect the Holy Book and prayer, the less we desire the Lord, and the further we drift away. Neglecting the daily and devotional study of the Scriptures, and spending less and less time in private prayer, the Lord becomes as a wilderness to us—nothing but a dry, unattractive, and thirsty land where no water is.

But wilderness places can blossom again. The wilderness and the solitary place can become places of gladness, and the desert can rejoice and blossom as the rose. One stanza old Dr. Tauler wrote, and it would be well for us to offer it as a prayer to our Lord and Saviour, as follows:

> *As the rose amid the briars*
> *Fresh and fair is found,*
> *Heedless of the tangled thicket,*
> *And the thorns around;*
> *As the sunflower ever turning*
> *To the mighty sun,*
> *With the faithfulness of fealty*
> *Following only One—*
> *SO MAKE ME, LORD, TO THEE!*

In this way we will practically enjoy these two blessed realities: *"That in all things He might have the pre-eminence." "That Christ may be all in all."*

Lovest Thou Me?

William Cowper

Hark, my soul! It is the Lord;
'Tis thy Saviour, hear His word;
Jesus speaks, and speaks to thee:
Say, poor sinner, lovest thou Me?

I delivered thee when bound,
And when bleeding, healed thy wound;
Sought thee wandering, set thee right,
Turned thy darkness into light.

Can a woman's tender care
Cease towards the child she bare?
Yes, she may forgetful be,
Yet will I remember thee.

Mine is an unchanging love,
Higher than the heights above;
Deeper than the depths beneath,
Free and faithful, strong as death.

Thou shalt see My glory soon,
When the work of grace is done;
Partner of my throne shalt be:
Say, poor sinner, lovest thou Me?

Lord, it is my chief complaint,
That my love is weak and faint;
Yet I love Thee and adore;
Oh for grace to love Thee more!

The Joy of the Way to Calvary

W. M. Clow

The way from Pilate's judgment seat to Calvary has been called the *Via Dolorosa*—the way of pain. If by that is meant that it was a way whose every step might well evoke our tears, whose simple record should renew and deepen our sorrow, the name is appropriate enough. But if the name be used to express the mind of Jesus, if it be His sorrow we have in view, its insight is at fault, and its use bestows no honor on Jesus. It is due to the Romish taint which has infected our thinking, and fastened our eyes on the physical sufferings of the cross, forgetful of what the reticence of the Gospels and the express triumph of the Epistles might have taught us—the radiant victory of the spirit over the flesh.

Jesus has been called the Man of Sorrows—outside the New Testament. The nearest approach in the Gospels to that name (which may mislead us if we are not careful) is the mention of the ignorant and mistaken conception that He was the prophet Jeremiah, a misconception Jesus at once brushes aside. The truth is that, in most of its aspects, Jesus lived a singularly joyous life. The most careless reader cannot escape feeling the calm and serenity of His words, and the perfect peace which pervades His life.

"Contentment" may express the high attainment of Paul, but it is too mean a word to apply to the life of Jesus; He had abounding joys. The silence that dwells among the lonely hills, the shadows on the Lake of Galilee, the array of the lilies, the glory of the grass of the field spoke to Him with a voice which no poet's ear ever heard. His delights were with the sons of men.

When we think of His incarnation, a shadow falls on our spirits as its humiliation forces itself upon us, but we forget the eager will behind it, which made its narrow limits a constant joy. His youth in

Nazareth...was a time of the leaping pulse and eager desire. His poverty—of which we, in our ignorance of an Eastern life, and our gluttony for ignoble comfort, have made too much—gave Him an unburdened life. *"A man's life,"* He said, *"consisteth not in the abundance of the things which he possesseth...Take no thought for the morrow."* Ah! when we understand the sources of joy, when we penetrate the secret of Jesus, we realize that, despite His loneliness and separateness in His higher experiences, despite the burden of men's sins and sorrows, and despite the last awful hour on the cross, no human heart ever thrilled with a joy to match that of Jesus.

When we regard Him closely as He passes up to Calvary, we find that from the depths of His joy a stream is flowing which cannot be quenched. Then we understand why He could say to His disciples, as He stood on the threshold of the agony of Gethsemane, and felt the very shadow of the cross: *"These things have I spoken unto you that My joy might remain in you, and that your joy might be full."*

Look at Jesus now as He walks the way to Calvary! The night—that searching and disciplining night for all who remained awake through its eventful hours—had passed away. Its festal joy and discerning love had found relief in the high priest's prayer after the supper. Its sleepless envy and craven fear have issued in the pitiless deeds of the courtyard and judgment seat.

Now the morning has ushered in the great day. Simon bears His cross, and now He is going forward to the last deed of all. A high elation is on His spirit, and a rush and surge of joyous feeling over mastering pain and quenching sorrow, swells in His heart. The wail of the women of Jerusalem breaks on His ear. He stops and turns, because He will not have them misunderstand Him, and give a false accompaniment to His crowning act. He chides them for their tears. The joys of sense have been taken from Him; of all the joys that man can take away, He has been bereaved. But He has the joys of the Spirit. He has His deep delight in spiritual things. And it was that inner, spiritual, eternal joy, welling up out of His victorious spirit, which made the way to Calvary an uplifting triumph.

Let us think about this joy of Jesus on the way to Calvary. Let us, under God's spirit, be guided into its knowledge and possession for so must we enter into His joy and so that our joy may be full.

The first source of Christ's joy lay in His SINLESSNESS. The great depth of the Old Testament Scripture is the judgment of God. His laws and ordinances are the marvel of the mind and heart. But the great depth of the New Testament is the sinlessness of Jesus. For all these centuries men have been plumbing it with the sounding lead of their speculation, and they have failed to fathom it. His words and deeds have been examined, tested, compared, and their spotless moral beauty has been made the more clear. *"Which man convinceth Me of sin?"* is the unanswered challenge of Christ. Today He stands unique; the one moral phenomenon, the one virgin life lived among men. When we contemplate the sinlessness of Jesus, it is as if we were looking up into the deep fathomless blue of heaven.

Of this joy of sinlessness you and I know nothing. The one fact, common to us all, is that we have sinned. But by our bitter experience we can faintly conceive what the lack of it may be. We have come to the hour of rest with the burden and shame of sin weighing down our hearts. We have awakened in the morning with the gnawing of remorse. We have felt the hot blush at the recollection of iniquities. We know how yet, at times, impulses of rebellion riot within us. And at all these times our joy is quenched. But when we have known ourselves purged from our iniquities, when we have cast out some lurking sin, when we have overcome and have put some temptation under our feet, then we have known the ministry of angels, and we have stood on the margin of Christ's joy.

But how meanly do these experiences image Christ's joy in His unspotted righteousness! Think of a conscience which had no accusing voice; of a spirit which had no burden of personal guilt; of a heart that never hungered after shameful wrong. Think of a soul that lived in the unclouded sunshine of the presence of God—so that no tears of shame for sin ever stained His cheek, and no broken, penitent prayer was ever on His lips. Now try to conceive the deep joy of a sinlessness like that. The happy, laughing innocence of a sunny child, compared to it, is but a world of shadows broken by light. As He goes to His cross, the sense of a life of sinlessness makes sunshine in His heart. As He goes upward to Calvary, the consciousness of a past of which He could say, *"I do always those things that please Him,"* and of a present whose difficult obedience He was fulfilling, is throbbing within Him, and He will not have even woman's tears misinterpret the rapture of His spirit. *"Thou lovest righteousness, and hatest wickedness; therefore, God, Thy God, hath anointed Thee with the oil of gladness above Thy fellows"* (Ps. 45:7).

Another source of Christ's joy lay in His SERVICE AND SACRIFICE. The idea of the joy of service, and of service which reaches to sacrifice, is commonly known. Yet how few of us believe it in our heart of hearts. The whole course of the conduct of men declares that it is when a man sits in state while other men serve him, when he receives abundant adulation, then his joy is full. Experience will not teach us the folly of it. The plainest evidence will not change this fleshly faith. Yet the truth is this—that it is in the hour of consecration to holy service, in the days of heroic self-denial, in the doing of the deed in which life itself is laid down, we experience that joy to which all others are but as poppies spread.

The soldiers who made the wild charge, and galloped into the jaws of death, had a deep joy in their obedience, such as they never know in the shelter of the bivouac. The man who has climbed the steep of a lonely sacrifice has an exquisite joy no words can express. There is one relationship in life which, as all of you can understand, calls supremely for service and sacrifice. That is motherhood. No one can compute the cost of the days and nights of waiting and watching, and the years of sacrifice a mother gives. But who will compute her joy in it all?

And when Jesus will tell His disciples how their service and sacrifice, wrought out in sorrow, will yield them joy, He has no higher image than the mother's joy in her sacrifice for her child. *"A woman, when she is in travail, hath sorrow, because her hour is come, but as soon as she is delivered of the child, she remembereth no more her anguish, for joy that a man is born into the world"* (Jn. 16:21). Has not your own experience brought this home to you? When you have accepted the burdens of your home; when you have gone down to the help of the needy, the sick, the poor, and the dying; when you made that sacrifice that left its mark on your life, you found a wellspring of joy, which has been a solace for almost every sorrow.

Think, then, what must have been Christ's joy in His HOLY SERVICE, IN HIS GREAT SACRIFICE. The joys of heaven did not so dilate His heart as the joy of the hour of His leaving them behind. The singing of the angels was only the sign of the joy of His spirit. And in every hour of His consecration, in every deed by which He made the children glad, or wiped away the tears of those who mourned, or healed the sick who were brought to Him, in every step forward towards His goal, He entered into His deep delight in spiritual things. And so, if you can realize it, this joy in His service and sacrifice was consummated on the way to Calvary.

In one way the day of the cross is the darkest, saddest, most tragic in the world's history. Yet it was the day of Christ's highest joy. As He goes up the way of weeping—spent, forsaken, marked for death—these women of Jerusalem lamented Him. He turned and looked upon them, and the triumph-song broke from His lips, *"Daughters of Jerusalem, weep not for Me...."* For He was going to the deed which crowned His life, He was accomplishing the purpose of His heart, He was on the threshold of His highest service and sacrifice, and His joy was almost full.

Ah, brethren, if you have ever felt the deep joy of making some poor wasted heart glad, if you have known the leaping of the spirit when some abandoned life has been saved from shame, if you have known the thrill when you have led some child to Christ, you can begin to realize what must have been the spiritual delight of the Son of God in that day when He died to set His people free.

The source of Christ's joy, I suggest, was His deep delight in the spiritual attainments of men. I venture to call this joy in the holiness and sanctification of men the highest of all, because it is the most spiritual and the most enduring. It is the joy in the presence of the angels over one sinner that repenteth. All great and Godlike souls have found this supreme joy in the spiritual well-being of others. It is Moses who prays that his name shall be blotted out of God's Book, rather than that His people Israel shall be cast away. It is Jonathan, that most captivating saint of the Old Testament, who can find his noblest joy in strengthening David's hand in God. It is Paul—great Paul—who cries: *"My heart's desire and prayer to God for Israel is that they may be saved...I could wish myself accursed from Christ, for my brethren, my kinsmen according to the flesh."* The man among us who has his deepest delight in the spiritual attainment of men, has pierced the secret of Jesus, will find a tireless energy in His service, can catch the throb of the holy passion in the words of Christ: *"These things have I spoken unto you that My joy might remain in you, and that your joy may be full,"* and can understand the elation of His spirit as He goes onward to His cross.

There is an incident in the life of Jesus that shows Him to us discriminating between the different joys that are possible to believing men. When the disciples returned from their tour in Galilee, they came to Him with joy, exclaiming that even the devils were subject to them. And Christ rejoiced with them. Yet, because He knew the subtle danger of all such sensational spiritual work, He said: *"Notwithstanding, in this rejoice not that the spirits are subject to you, but rather rejoice that your names are written in heaven."* Then we read: *"In that hour Jesus Himself rejoiced in spirit, and said: I thank Thee, O Father, Lord of heaven and earth, that Thou hast hid these things from the wise and prudent, and hast revealed them unto babes."* There is thus the joy in the triumph of spiritual work, and the joy in the assurance of the mercy of God, and the joy in the knowledge of the spiritual attainments of men. This joy is highest of all.

This was the joy that made the bright days of His life. The pity of it is that He passed so many wintry days—that so often He would have blessed men, but they would not. When the rich young ruler went away sorrowful, he left a still more sorrowful heart behind him. When Christ beheld the city that did not know the day of its visitation, He wept. When Judas went out, and it was night, and shut the door of mercy upon himself, he shadowed Christ's longing heart.

But Jesus had hours of joy. When Andrew and John sought Him, and sat all night at His feet; when Matthew left his custom-box to follow Him; when Zaccheus' long-bound heart burst within him Jesus entered into His joy. When the woman of Samaria drank of the water of life, He had meat to eat that the world knew not of. When the woman who was a sinner came behind and kissed His feet, and wiped them with her hair, Simon's bread lay untasted on the table. And when Mary's oil was poured upon Him, His joy was full—for He saw within a woman's soul the beauty of His own grace reflected. He saw the will of God done on earth as it is done in heaven.

And now, as He sees the beams which shall make His cross, as He is fulfilling the eternal sacrifice, as He is within a few hours of the moment when He shall cry, *"It is finished,"* and then go home, His joy is greater than human heart can conceive. What word could have been more suitable on His lips to these compassionate daughters of Jerusalem, what word is to be spoken yet to men among us who dwell overmuch on the sorrows of the way, but *"Weep not for Me"*? The joy in the spiritual well-being of men still throbs in the human heart that beats on the throne of God.

He still *"sees of the travail of His soul"* and is satisfied. Not only when He saw Peter's impulsive soul chastened into steadfast strength; not only when He saw John's fiery heart glowing with love; not only when He saw Thomas's doubting spirit strengthened in faith; but today when He sees our faces turned towards Him, when He sees us laying aside all malice, and all guile, and all hypocrisies, and envies and evil speaking; when He sees us overcoming by faith. This is *"the joy set before Him,"* for which He endured the cross and despised the shame, the joy which shall be fulfilled, "when all the ransomed Church of God is saved to sin no more."

He ennobles all the pure joys of earth. But He continually tells us that these are not the highest possible to the spirit of a man. He tells us that these are the joys which may be taken away. The highest joy—the joy He would have remain in you—is this deep delight in spiritual things which throbbed in His heart on the way to Calvary.

Into that joy we enter as He entered. We cannot have the joy of sinlessness. But we can possess that joy which, for guilty, sin-stained men, corresponds to it—the joy of pardon, of peace with God, of complete surrender to His will. We can have the joy of service and sacrifice. The world around us is stretching out its withered hands to be healed, its empty hearts to be filled. And we can have that purest, holiest joy, into which no subtle selfishness enters, in the spiritual well-being of men. These made the joy of the way to Calvary. As we enter into this joy of Jesus we shall find it quenching all desire for base and degrading pleasures, fitting us for our solemn hours of trial, satisfying our spirits in the years when all other delights may pall, and preparing us for that hour of awakening in His presence. It is a blessing which maketh rich and addeth no sorrow, an earnest of the pleasures which are at God's right hand for evermore.

The Song of His Joy

Frances Beven

Wondrous joy, Thy joy, Lord Jesus,
Deep eternal, pure, and bright—
Thou alone the Man of Sorrows
Thus could tell of joy aright.

Lord, we know that joy, that gladness,
Which in fullness Thou hast given—
Sharing all the countless treasure,
We on earth with Thee in heaven.

Even as He went before us
Through the wilderness below,
So in strength unworn, unfailing,
Onward also would we go.

All the earth a desert round Him,
All His springs in God alone;
Every heart, save God's heart only,
Making discord with His own.

There to walk alone, rejoicing—
Through the ruin and the sin;
Darkness of the midnight round Him
Glory of God's love within.

From no lower fountain flowing
Than the heart of God above,
All the gladness of that glory,
All the power of that love.

Onward to the cross rejoicing
Where the powers of evil met
Giving thanks midst deepest darkness
That God's love was deeper yet.

Then ascended in the glory,
By that love's unfailing spring,
There to sing the song of triumph,
There the song of songs to sing.

Hearken to that hymn of glory
Filling all the holy place,
Golden psalm of Him who looketh
On the Father's blessed face.

Voice of measureless rejoicing,
Joy unmingled, deep and clear,
Wonder to the listening heavens,
Music to the Father's ear.

Won in travail of His spirit,
Agony, and shame, and blood,
That blest place beside the Father,
Nearest to the heart of God.

Won for me! My praises leading,
Jesus sings that song divine;
All His joy my own forever,
All His peace forever mine.

What though drought be all around me,
Desert land on every side—
With that spring of love and gladness
Shall I not be satisfied?

Never Man Spake Like This Man

George Goodman

Four simple men were used by God to record the history of One who called Himself the Son of Man, who walked familiarly among men, eating and drinking, and conversing with them. They tell their story in plain, straightforward language, each in his own style, scarcely commenting on what is recorded, but writing as those who narrate what they saw, and tell what they heard.

There are too many marks of diversity to allow that they were in collusion; yet it is the same divine Person who is depicted, who speaks in the same marvellous way. It is impossible to conceive that four ordinary men, writing separately, could each have invented such a perfect character or could have put such words into His lips.

Matthew, the publican; Mark, the servant; Luke, the physician; and John, the fisherman, record for us in a candid and open manner the words of Him who spoke as *"never man spoke."*

The words themselves, as recorded, are comparatively few. We have no long dissertations, no elaborate treatises. The longest discourse takes but fifteen minutes to read aloud. The whole of His words could, I suppose, be printed in a pamphlet of sixteen pages, and yet those words are such that they have astounded the whole world, and established His reputation. *"The same is a Perfect Man."* More than this, *"Truly this was the Son of God."*

There is no spot or blemish in them, no confession of sin, no mistake, no uncertainty, no hesitation. Such terms as "Perhaps," "I think," "It is possibly so," or other evidence of fallibility is indiscoverable. All is authoritative, calm, and decisive: *"I say unto you."*

The style is perfect. Not a vestige appears of sentimentality, no weak emotion, no plea for pity, no mock heroics, no posing for effect, no lightness or trifling, no irritation or hastiness. There is no

dead fly in the ointment to mar His reputation for wisdom.

These four writers hold up for admiration nothing that the world gloried in. It is doubtful if they had any thought of depicting a hero or great man—they told a simple story of One whom they had seen and loved, and whose words had reached their hearts.

Let us look at this collection of His words. We need not be enthusiasts or devotees, we need bring no prejudice, nor look at it through colored glasses. It bears examination. It seems to say to all: *"I speak as to wise men, judge ye what I say"* (1 Cor. 10:15). Let us judge this unique volume first from the lowest of men's standards.

HIS WORDS AS ORDINARY LITERATURE

We discover at once that here is narration unequalled in the world. Read the parable of the Prodigal Son. It has attained worldwide fame. Note its simple pathos, its powerful appeal to the heart. Tears of thousands have been shed on the pages. It has turned untold sinners to a new life. In order to test its excellence by comparison, search through all the great writers of the world for something to compare with it for simplicity, dignity, and excellence.

In the Greek it contains but 396 words, not one of which could be spared as mere verbiage. Can Shakespeare, Milton, Dante, Goethe, Longfellow or Wordsworth or any of our prose authors supply anything to compete with it? But the same gracious lips told the story of the Lost Sheep; the Good Samaritan; the parable of the Sower; the Publican and the Pharisee; the Great Supper for the poor, blind, and lame; the Ten Virgins; and the Rich Man and Lazarus. Where in all the field of literature shall we find anything to compare with, much more to surpass, these masterpieces of literary art?

Who is this that at once steps above all the world's greatest writers, to be acknowledged superior to them all? Surely judged by this lowest of standards, *"never man spake like this Man."*

Now let us judge His words by another standard.

THE MORAL EXCELLENCE OF HIS WORDS

There have been many moralists in the world, and many codes of honor, and much sound advice as to conduct. Good moral teaching has been the common property of the sages of the past, but which of them can compare with the exalted wisdom and heart-searching purity of the Sermon on the Mount?

The ideals that have been held up to men for their admiration and emulation are quietly set aside. The warrior in shining armor gives place to the blessedness of the gentle, the merciful, to the love of enemies and a desire to do them good. The accumulation of wealth is rebuked as not representing truly that in which a man's life consists, rather it is in giving and lending, while no return is looked for. The heavenly Father will supply the present need and the reward will be in heaven, with not even *"the cup of cold water"* forgotten.

The pride of religious display and love of applause are rebuked. Prayer, fasting, giving are only means to an end, and that end not self, but communion with God, and loving thought for others.

The searching demand for purity that is of the heart, that governs even the restless eyes; and the love that regards hatred as murder; the obedience that hears and does, and thus builds the life on a foundation of rock. Such is the exalted morality that places the words of Christ out of reach of any competitor, and causes us still to exclaim, *"He taught as One having authority!"*

Think, too, of the sympathy and encouragement contained in His words. Moralists are confessedly stern men, hard in their words and harsh in their judgments. But this Man, though His words are often weighty in their burden, He was never accused of being cold, harsh, or unfeeling. Even the chapter of *"Woes"* (in Mt. 23) ends with tender words of compassion: *"O Jerusalem, Jerusalem, thou that killest the prophets, and stonest them which are sent unto thee, how often would I have gathered thy children together, even as a hen gathereth her chickens under her wings, and ye would not!"* (Mt. 23:37).

The common people heard Him gladly, marvelling at His gracious words. Sinners wept at His feet, the brokenhearted were comforted and their wounds bound up. Did ever man speak to sinners as He? *"Thy sins be forgiven,"* *"Go in peace,"* yet with no laxity of morals. *"Go, and sin no more."*

But we have to recognize in this Volume of His words greater marvels than those. It is impossible to close our eyes to the fact that in His words we find the most stupendous claims and a self-assertion that is beyond anything in knowledge or experience.

HE PREACHED HIMSELF

He claimed to be the Salvation He came to bring. His use of the words "I AM" was equivalent to the assumption of deity. It identified Him with Jehovah who appeared in the burning bush—the *"I Am that I Am"*—and stirred the wrath of the Pharisees, who accused Him of *"making Himself equal with God"* (Jn. 5:18), a charge which He did not refute, but confirmed by the words, *"All men should honor the Son, even as they honor the Father"* (Jn. 5:23).

The Jews knew and loved Psalm 23 dearly, as any Christian does. *"Jehovah is my Shepherd."* What then must have been their feelings when they heard this Man say, *"I am the Good Shepherd"* (Jn. 10:11)? They knew that this involved a claim to be Jehovah.

The "I AM" was constantly on His lips. *"Before Abraham was, I AM"* (Jn. 8:58). *"When ye have lifted up the Son of Man then shall ye know that I AM"* (Jn. 8:28). *"If ye believe not that I AM, ye shall die in your sins"* (Jn. 8:24). Perhaps the most remarkable use of the words was in the garden when they came to take Him. *"Whom seek ye?...Jesus of Nazareth. Jesus saith unto them, I AM...As soon then as He had said unto them I AM, they went backwards and fell to the ground"* (Jn. 18:4-6). His words overpowered them.

As we ponder such words, we can only exclaim with Simeon, *"Mine eyes have seen Thy salvation"* (Lk. 2:30). Is a sinner seeking access to God? He says, *"I am the Door, by Me if any man enter in, he shall be saved"* (Jn. 10:9). Is a hungry soul longing for satisfaction? He says, *"I am that Bread of Life"* (Jn. 6:48). Does one long to know his way Home through the darkness? He says, *"I am the Light of the world"* (Jn. 8:12). Is one troubled with the confusion of voices in this Babylon with its higher critics, its philosophers, its modernists? He quiets the strife with the word, *"I am the Truth."* Does one long for nourishment for the soul that shall produce fruit in the life? He says, *"I am the Vine, ye are the branches"* (Jn. 15:5). Does one want assurance? He says, *"I am the Good Shepherd...My sheep...shall never perish"* (Jn. 10:14, 28). Do men tremble by the open grave? Then hear His words, matchless above all that even He spoke, *"I am the Resurrection and the Life, he that believeth in Me, though he were dead, yet shall he live"* (Jn. 11:25).

Thus did He claim to be the only Saviour. For any other to use such language was to expose himself to ridicule. Yet *"this Man"* used the words with authority and undiminished dignity and grace.

Now notice His claim as the great Rest-giver. Did ever man use such words as these? *"Come unto Me, all ye that labor and are heavy laden, and I will give you rest"* (Mt. 11:28)? Many teachers in the past have exhorted men to take their advice; to carry out their laws; even to follow their example; but who among the sons of men ever said, *"Come unto Me, and I will give you rest"*?

A Christian distributing tracts in France gave a text on a card to a gentleman, who read it curiously. It had on it the words, *"Come unto Me, all ye that labor and are heavy laden, and I will give you rest."* There was no indication who had said those words, and the reader showed some surprise that he should be invited by a stranger in such terms. Looking at him earnestly, he said, "Well, here I am!" What a dilemma! It took some time to explain *Who* it was that could give men such an invitation, for no man spake like this Man.

Hear also this claim to deity—He answers prayer! *"If ye shall ask anything in My Name, I will do it"* (Jn. 14:14). Who is this whose Name is so powerful, who Himself answers prayer: *"I will do it"*?

He claims to raise and judge all men: *"Many shall say to Me in that day, Lord, Lord"* (Mt. 7:22). Who would dare to speak thus? Or, *"The hour is coming in the which all that are in the graves shall hear His voice, and shall come forth; they that have done good, unto the resurrection of life; and they that have done evil, unto the resurrection of damnation"* (Jn. 5:28-29). In fact He claims life itself. Think of this worldwide demand: *"If any man come to Me, and hate not his father, and mother, and wife, and children, and brethren, and sisters, yea, and his own life also, he cannot be My disciple"* (Lk. 14:26). Who is entitled to make such a claim as this? Never man spake like this! We can not only wonder at the claim, but at the greater wonder that, down through the ages, millions have accorded it to Him, for never has man been so loved as this Man, never have life and possessions been so willingly sacrificed for other, as for His sake. Truly this is the Son of God. And sweetest of all words to His own, *"this Man"* who ever liveth, has said, *"I will come again and receive you unto Myself."* *"Even so, come, Lord Jesus."*

The Everlasting Word

Josiah Conder

Thou art the everlasting Word,
The Father's only Son;
God manifestly seen and heard,
And heaven's beloved One.

In Thee most perfectly expressed,
The Father's glories shine;
Of the full deity possessed,
Eternally divine.

True Image of the Infinite,
Whose essence is concealed;
Brightness of uncreated light,
The heart of God revealed.

But the high mysteries of His name
The angel's grasp transcend;
The Father only (glorious claim!)
The Son can comprehend.

Yet loving Thee, on whom His love
Ineffable doth rest,
Thy members all, below, above,
As one with Thee, are blest.

Throughout the universe of bliss,
The center Thou, and Sun;
Th' eternal theme of praise is this,
To heaven's beloved One.

Worthy, O Lamb of God, art Thou,
That every knee to Thee should bow.

Sorrow and Gladness

W. Bramwell Dick

How deeply touching are the words of our Lord Jesus: *"My soul is exceeding sorrowful"* (Mt. 26:38). We do well to meditate upon them, because while our hearts overflow with praise as we recall what He has done, our spirits are subdued; and while we exult in all the blessing that He has secured for us, we are humbled as we remember what it cost Him. We approach this hallowed spot with unshod feet and with reverent hearts. Leaving the upper room, the blessed Lord, accompanied by the eleven, went to Gethsemane. There He said, *"Sit ye here, while I go and pray yonder"* (v. 36). That was a spot beyond their reach, beyond their understanding. Then He took three who seemed to be a little nearer than the others, but to them He said, *"Tarry ye here...and He went a little farther"* (vv. 38-39). They had reached the utmost limit, just as we do when we meditate upon His sorrow, and we seem to hear a voice saying, *"Hitherto shalt thou come, but no farther"* (Job 38:11).

We are reminded of the beautiful picture in Genesis 22 where Abraham went to offer up Isaac. On the third day, he *"saw the place afar off,"* and *"said unto his young men, Abide ye here... and I and the lad will go yonder...And they went both of them together"* (vv. 4-6). Then came Isaac's question and the father's answer; once more we read: *"And they went both of them together"* (v. 6).

In the garden, the Father and the Son "went both of Them together." The Son was *"exceeding sorrowful,"* and if the disciples so little entered into it that they slept, the Father knew it. But oh, His love! If, in the perfection of His holiness, He shrank from the cup, in the perfection of His obedience He took it, and, at the cross in the perfection of His love He "drained the last dark drop."

Precious Saviour, we worship Thee! Sorrowing saint, are you

crushed and overwhelmed with grief? He was *"exceeding sorrowful."* Is the cup that has been pressed to your lips bitter? Never could a cup be as bitter as that which the Father placed in His hand. Today you have at your service everything that you need in the One who for your sake was *"exceeding sorrowful."*

In Psalm 21:6, we see the answer: *"Thou hast made Him exceeding glad with Thy countenance."* We follow Him from the garden of Gethsemane through "death's dark vale," on to resurrection triumph. We look up to the throne of God and see Him there with *"a crown of pure gold on His head"* (v. 3), and with *"honor and majesty laid upon Him"* (v. 5). We see Him set there to be *"blessings forever"* (v. 6, marg.). All this is the result of His having been *"exceeding sorrowful,"* and, as He surveys it, He is *"exceeding glad."* *"Weeping may endure for a night, but joy cometh in the morning"* (Ps. 30:5). His night of weeping has ended, and He has entered upon the morning of everlasting joy.

We could have no part in His sorrow. Alone He had to bear that, and, blessed be His name, He did bear it. It is our happy privilege, however, to be sharers of His joy. How He delights to share that with us! Yet His joy is always the greatest. If we find joy in being gathered together around Him, and we feel like the disciples of whom it is recorded, *"Then were the disciples glad, when they saw the Lord"* (Jn. 20:20), His joy in having us near Him is even greater. If our joy will be unspeakable when He comes for us and takes us to be with Him in the Father's House, His joy will be infinitely greater. He shall present us *"faultless before the presence of His glory with exceeding joy"* (Jude 24). The Father has so ordered things that *"in all things He might have the preeminence"* (Col. 1:18). He was preeminent in sorrow in the garden and on the cross, even as in His pathway He was *"a Man of sorrows, and acquainted with grief"* (Isa. 53:3). Yet He is also preeminent in the gladness that fills His heart today. And He will be preeminent in the joy that shall be His in the coming day of glory.

The Sweetener of Marah's Waters

Fanny J. Crosby

Not always on the mountain
The sweetest flowers we find,
But sometimes in the valley,
With cypress branches twined.
We see their buds unclosing,
Their blossoms bending low,
A hallowed fragrance breathing
Where Marah's waters flow.

O valley of submission,
Where once the Son of God,
Our precious, loving Saviour,
In lonely silence trod.
And when our hearts are breaking,
To Him we there may go,
Assured that He is nearest,
Where Marah's waters flow.

O valley of submission,
Where, leaning on His breast,
We tell Him all our sorrow,
And feel the calm of rest.
Tho' oft He gently leads us,
Where verdant pastures grow
His Mercy shines the brightest
Where Marah's waters flow.

The Claims of Christ

W. H. Griffith Thomas

J ust as a diamond has several facets, each one contributing to the beauty and attractiveness of the complete stone, so Christ can be considered in various ways; to the question, *"What think ye of Christ?"* different answers can be given. Looking again at the Gospel story of His life, we are conscious of one remarkable fact that stands out on almost every page, from the beginning to the close of His ministry. This is the claim that He made for Himself. It was a fivefold claim of a far-reaching nature.

HE CLAIMED TO BE THE MESSIAH OF THE JEWS. It is well known that the Old Testament is a book of expectation, and that it closes with the expectation very largely unrealized. The Jews as a nation were always looking forward to the coming of a great personage whom they called the Messiah. He would fulfill all their prophecies, realize all their hopes, and accomplish all their designs for themselves and for the world. Jesus Christ of Nazareth claimed to be this Messiah. During His ministry He referred to many passages in the Old Testament and pointed to Himself as the explanation and application of it. He took the Jewish law and claimed not only to fulfill it but to give it a wider, fuller, and deeper meaning. *"I came not to destroy, but to fulfill."* It was Jesus' definite claim to be the Messiah that led in great part to the opposition shown to Him by the Jews.

HE CLAIMED TO BE IN SOME WAY THE REDEEMER, to *"seek and to save that which was lost"; "The Son of man came not to be ministered unto, but to minister, and to give His life a ransom for many."* This description of men as *"lost,"* i.e., helpless, useless, and in danger of future condemnation, and this statement about His having come to *"save"* them, constitute a claim that implies uniqueness of relation to humanity.

HE CLAIMED TO BE THE MASTER OF MANKIND. He said that He was the Lord of the Sabbath. He called for obedience from men by His definite, all-embracing command, *"Follow Me."* The earliest influence of Christ over His disciples was exercised quite naturally and simply, and yet the claim He made on them was absolute. But the narrative nowhere suggests that they felt it to be unwarranted. It is recorded without any explanation or justification, as though He had a perfect right to make it. The words are so familiar that we may fail to realize their astounding and far-reaching character. Think of what they mean. *"He that loveth father or mother more than Me is not worthy of Me." "He that loseth his life for My sake shall find it."* This remarkable claim to His right to control lives and to be the supreme motive in life is surely more than human. He preached the kingdom of God and announced Himself as the King.

Still more, HE CLAIMED TO BE THE JUDGE OF MANKIND. He said that His words should judge mankind at the last day, and more than once He depicted Himself as the judge before whom all men should be gathered to receive their reward or punishment. He claimed to sum up all the past and to decide all the future.

Above all, HE CLAIMED NOTHING LESS THAN THE PREROGATIVES OF GOD. He claimed to be able to forgive sins, eliciting from His enemies a charge of blasphemy. They reasoned, *"Who can forgive sins but God?"* He claimed God's work when He said, *"My Father worketh hitherto, and I work."* He told the Jews that all things had been delivered to Him by His Father, and because of this He invited all that labored and were heavy laden to come to Him for rest. The words of Matthew 11 call for the closest study. *"All things are delivered unto Me of My Father: and no man knoweth the Son, but the Father; neither knoweth any man the Father, save the Son, and he to whomsoever the Son will reveal Him. Come unto Me, all ye that labor and are heavy laden, and I will give you rest."* The obvious interpretation of this statement is that Christ was conscious of a unique relation to God and of a unique relation to man based on it.

Is not this the New Testament picture of Jesus Christ? Can any one doubt as he reads the four Gospels, or even the first three Gospels, that this, and nothing short of it, is the claim that He made for Himself as Messiah, Redeemer, Master, Judge, and God?

But we cannot stop with a general consideration of these remarkable claims; we must endeavor to discover whether they are warranted. To claim is one thing; to justify and vindicate the claim is quite another. Character and deeds must bear the strain of this stupendous claim to be unique in relation to God and man.

That Jesus believed Himself to be the Messiah is a fact that emerges from a careful reading of the Gospels. It is evident that Christ was conscious of His Messiahship at His baptism (Mt. 3:15). The name Messiah was frequently applied to Jesus by others. There are three occasions on which He accepted it for Himself (Mt. 16:16-17; Mk. 14:61-62; Jn. 4:25-26). And although He refused from time to time to reveal Himself to the Jews, who were only too ready to mistake His words and oppose His claim, the evidence of the Gospels is far too weighty to allow any denial of the Messiahship of Jesus Christ as claimed, allowed, and implied by Him.

> Some critics have called in question the fact that Jesus called Himself Messiah. But this article of evangelical tradition seems to me to stand the test of the most minute investigation.[1]

> Historically considered, the calling which Jesus embraced, and with which was bound up His significance for the world, was and could be no other than to be the Messiah of His people.[2]

This divine consciousness is all the more remarkable when it is considered against the background of His perfect humility. We see Him proclaiming and exemplifying meekness on every possible occasion. But if His claims were untrue, is there not something here that is not merely egotism but blasphemy?

> It is doubly surprising to observe that these enormous pretensions were advanced by one whose special peculiarity, not only among His contemporaries, but among the remarkable men that have appeared before and since, was an almost feminine in tenderness and humility. Yet so clear to Him was His own dignity and infinite importance to the human race as an objective fact with which His own opinion of Himself had nothing to do, that in the same breath in which He asserts it in the most unmeasured language, He alludes, apparently with entire unconsciousness, to His own humility: "I am meek and lowly."[3]

Since, too, He claimed to bring God to man in a definite and unique way, and to bestow such grace as would transform and uplift man's life, the question naturally arises whether such an One as Jesus Christ would arouse hopes in man that He could not satisfy.

> Bronson Alcott once said to Carlyle that he could honestly use the words of Jesus, *"I and the Father are one."* "Yes," was the crushing retort, "but Jesus got the world to believe Him."[4]

And so we have to face and explain this divine consciousness of Christ. Was ever a human being seen like this? A Man exemplifying the passive virtues combined with unique majesty. A Man challenging attention to His sinlessness and meekness, and yet obviously sincere. A Man claiming unlimited power, and yet ever expressing His dependence on God. A Man possessed of undaunted courage, and yet characterized by exceptional meekness. A Man interested in the smallest details of individual lives, and yet conscious of possessing universal relations with God and man. A Man deeply impressed with the awful realities and consequences of human sin, and yet ever possessed by a sunny optimism which faced the facts and looked forward to sin's eternal destruction. A Man born and educated amid narrow and narrowing Jewish tradition, and yet characterized by an originality and a universality which rises infinitely above all national and racial limits. A Man of perfect humility, absolute sincerity, entire sinlessness, and yet all the while actually asserting Himself to be humble, sincere, and sinless.

> A young man who had not long left the carpenter's workshop, who at the moment He spoke was in a condition of poverty, and was associated only with those who were obscure and poor like Himself, calmly declared His sense of perfect faultlessness and of extraordinary relation to God.[5]

What are we to say in the face of these astonishing claims? How are we to reconcile this self-assertion on the one hand with that high degree of personal character and excellence which all men, friends and foes, have accorded to Jesus Christ throughout the ages? How is it that these claims which would be absolutely intolerable in any other man have been allowed and almost universally accepted in the case of Jesus Christ?

Surely there is only one conclusion to all this; either Jesus Christ

is God, or else He is not a good man. "If it is not superhuman authority that speaks to us here, it is surely superhuman arrogance."[6] There
is no middle path. Either Jesus Christ is God or else He is utterly
undeserving of our thought and regard.

We therefore find ourselves face to face with the problem of how
to account for the Person, life, and character of Jesus of Nazareth.
As has been forcibly pointed out, the ordinary factors of life cannot
possibly account for Him. Race, family, place, time, education,
opportunity—these are the six ordinary factors of human life, and
they can all be examined without any of them, or even all of them
together, accounting for Jesus Christ.[7] Everything in Him is at once
perfectly natural and yet manifestly supernatural. He is unique in the
history of mankind. As Bishop Gore has well said,

> One man of a particular race and age cannot be the standard for all men, the
> judge of all men, of all ages and races, the goal of human, moral development,
> unless he is something more than one man among many. Such a universal
> Manhood challenges inquiry.[8]

This inquiry Christianity invites all men to pursue. Jesus Christ
cannot be ignored. Whenever human thought has endeavored to do
this, it has been found impossible. Whenever human life now tries to
do so, the task is soon seen to be beyond it. He must be considered.
He demands the attention of all true men. The supreme question
today, as ever, is *"What think ye of Christ?"*

—*Christianity is Christ,* (Chicago, IL: Moody Press, 1965) pp. 19-30.

ENDNOTES:

1 W. Sanday, *Life of Christ in Recent Research,* p. 137

2 J. Weiss, *Life of Christ,* I, p. 195

3 J. H. B. Masterman, *Was Jesus Christ Divine?* p. 63

4 *Religion and the Modern Mind,* David Smith, "The Divinity of Jesus," p. 167

5 J. Young, *The Christ of History,* p. 211

6 *An Appeal to Unitarians,* quoted by Charles Gore, *The Incarnation* (Bamton
Lectures) p. 238

7 Fairbairn, *Philosophy of the Christian Religion,* pp. 311-312

8 Bishop Gore, *The Incarnation,* p. 25

Peerless Worth

Ora Rowan (1834-1879)

Hast thou heard Him, seen Him, known Him?
Is not thine a captured heart?
Chief among ten thousand own Him,
Gladly choose the better part.

Idols once they won thee, charmed thee,
Lovely things of time and sense;
Gilded, thus does sin disarm thee,
Honey'd, lest thou turn thee thence.

What has stripped the seeming beauty
From the idols of the earth?
Not the sense of right or duty,
But the sight of peerless worth.

Not the crushing of those idols,
With its bitter void and smart;
But the beaming of His beauty,
The unveiling of His heart.

Who extinguishes his taper
'Till he hails the rising sun?
Who discards the garb of winter
'Till the summer has begun?

'Tis the look that melted Peter,
'Tis the face that Stephen saw,
'Tis the heart that wept with Mary,
Can alone from idols draw.

Draw and win and fill completely,
Till the cup o'erflow the brim:
What have we to do with idols,
Who have companied with Him?

Shadows of Christ

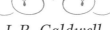

J. R. Caldwell

Doubtless there is much to be known of God in creation. The invisible things of God (Rom. 1:20) are clearly seen, *"even His eternal power and Godhead."* That which could be known of God they cared not to know, and, instead of acknowledging their ignorance, they professed to be wise—therefore were they fools, and God gave them up to their folly.

But God's purpose to reveal Himself was not to be frustrated, either by sin or man's unwillingness to know Him. The revelation of Himself is of interest to a wider circle than to man or this world. When earth was created, there were unfallen beings who discerned in its creation His eternal power and Godhead. It was so far a revelation of Himself. And as they beheld a fair creation spring into being, ordered and completed by His word, *"The morning stars sang together, and all the sons of God shouted for joy"* (Job 38:7).

Even fallen man might have apprehended this from creation, but he would not. He did not like to retain God in his knowledge. Hence the science (falsely so called) of the present day, with all its heritage of the learning of ages past, doubts if there be a God at all, denies creation, and substitutes a theory of development and natural laws for God. But after all, creation with all its glory tells only of His power and Godhead.

Providence tells jointly with the voice of creation that God is good. He did not leave Himself without a witness—in that He did them good—giving them fruitful seasons, *"Filling [their] hearts with food and gladness"* (Acts 14:17). He makes His sun to shine upon the evil and the good, and His rain to fall on the just and the unjust. Thus again He partially reveals Himself, going further than to show His power and Godhead. He gives a little glimpse of His mercifulness and goodness. To this man is also blind. He glorifies Him not as God neither is thankful (Rom. 1:21).

But yet there was that in God which was unrevealed. Deep in the bosom of God was hidden the unopened fountain of grace. To unseal this fountain, to display this wondrous attribute of the character of God in its fullness, to show it in combination with and in harmony with all His other attributes, was from eternity the purpose of God. It was before creation, for before the foundation of the world the Lamb was foreordained for sacrifice, so that creation and the fall—the entrance of Satan and of sin into the first creation, with all its terrible results, its confusion, its havoc, and ruin—are only so many stages towards the great platform whereon God was about to reveal Himself, in a fullness infinitely surpassing all revelations that had ever gone before.

Herein lies the ultimate design of the stupendous mystery of the incarnation, the sacrifice, the resurrection, and the glorifying of the Son of God. To save a lost and guilty people was a purpose worthy of God, but even this is not the ultimate design. Rather it is *"that, in the ages to come, He might show the exceeding riches of His grace in His kindness towards us through Christ Jesus"* (Eph. 2:7). It is the complete revelation of Himself; the opening out, of the very heart of God, that He, the Unknown, might be known—that, being known, He might be loved with an ever-deepening love, and praised with a fuller and higher joy by every unfallen and redeemed being.

Oh, the deep, deep meaning of that word uttered by the only One who had fully known God, who knew Him by dwelling from eternity in His very bosom. *"This is life eternal, that they might know Thee, the only true God, and Jesus Christ whom Thou hast sent"* (Jn. 17:3). It is life eternal to know God; not to know Him is death.

It has pleased God, therefore, to make Himself known, to reveal or discover Himself in the Person of His Son. He is *"the brightness of [God's] glory, and the express image of His person"* (Heb. 1:3). *"God manifested in the flesh"* (1 Tim. 3:16). So perfectly, so accurately represented to us, that He could say, in answer to Philip's question, *"show us the Father,"* *"Have I been so long time with you, and hast thou not known Me, Philip? He that hath seen Me, hath seen the Father"* (Jn. 14:9). But the natural man has not the capacity to comprehend even the perfect manifestation which God has given of Himself in His Son. *"He was in the world, and the world knew Him not. He came to His own, and His own received Him not"* (Jn. 1:10-11). *"Had they known, they would not have crucified the Lord of glory"* (1 Cor. 2:8). It has been well remarked that the flesh of Christ was that which veiled and yet revealed the Godhead. It was a veil so thick that the carnal eye could not penetrate it. The natural man only saw in Him *"a root out of a dry ground,"* a man with visage marred, the son of Mary and Joseph, the carpenter of Nazareth.

But through that veil of flesh there shone with holy, tempered radiance a glory such as faith could discern. *"And we beheld His glory, the glory as of the only begotten of the Father, full of grace and truth"* (Jn. 1:14). To the opened eye, He was God manifest in the flesh, Immanuel, God with us.

But the Word made flesh is no longer on earth. We see Him not, though we love Him. In the meantime, there is given to us the written Word and the Holy Spirit who takes of the things of Christ and shows them to us (Jn. 16:13-14). We are thus not left without a Comforter; in fact it was expedient for the disciples that Christ should go away, that the other Comforter should come. Through His teaching and anointing they should know more of Christ than had He remained with them on earth. And it is through the written Word that the Spirit of God ministers Christ to the souls of His people, for there has God with infinite skill treasured up for us His Christ, giving us every lineament of His character, every detail of His work, His sufferings, and His glory, every relationship that He bears to God, to His saints, and to the sinner. No mere historical record could accomplish this, no biography ever attempted it—the idea is God's.

To effect this, He has therefore resorted to a great variety of methods in the Word to reveal Christ. There is the purely historical record of the four Gospels, giving us Christ as seen by man among men—His outward life as He passed before the world and His disciples. Then there are the Prophetic Scriptures in the Old Testament, to which the book of Revelation in the New might almost be regarded as an appendix and a key. These give the official glories of Christ as the Heir, and a glimpse here and there at the sufferings through which He acquired the glory.

Distinct from these stands the Book of Psalms, wherein we are brought, as it were, to listen to the very breathings, to feel the very throbbings of the heart of Christ in the midst of those sorrows, temptations, and agonies, that were relieved by no human sympathy.

This is the way God has taken to lead His beloved and highly-privileged children into a nearness and intimacy with the only begotten Son, into which no biography, however detailed—not even a personal acquaintance on earth—could have introduced them. To this class belong the book of Lamentations and the Song of Solomon—the one giving the sorrows and the other the joys, that found no outward expression among men, and therefore could not find a place in the history of His outward walk given in the Gospels.

Finally there are the types and shadows of the law, and many personal pictures in which Christ was set forth so vividly ages before He appeared on the earth, that no reasonable and unbiased mind could come to any other conclusion than that these overshadowings are indeed divine.

These constitute a picture gallery of our Lord Jesus Christ, in which every aspect of His work and of His personal suitability for it, of His atonement and His priestly intercession, are abundantly unveiled and explained. May the eyes of our understanding be enlightened in the knowledge of Him.

—*Shadows of Christ* (Glasgow: Pickering and Inglis, n.d.), pp. 12-17.

The Eternal Generation of the Son

Frederick William Faber

Amid the eternal silences
God's endless Word was spoken;
None heard but He who always spake,
And the silence was unbroken.

For ever in the eternal land
The glorious day is dawning;
For ever is the Father's light
Like an endless outspread morning.

From the Father's vast tranquility,
In light coequal glowing
The kingly consubstantial Word
Is unutterably flowing.

For ever climbs that Morning Star
Without ascent or motion;
For ever as its daybreak shed
On the Spirit's boundless ocean.

O Word! Who fitly can adore
Thy Birth and Thy relation,
Lost in the impenetrable light
Of Thine awful Generation?

Thy Father clasps Thee evermore
In unspeakable embraces,
While angels tremble as they praise
And shroud their dazzled faces.

And oh! in what abyss of love,
So fiery yet so tender,
The Holy Ghost encircles Thee
With His uncreated splendor!

O Word! O dear and gentle Word!
Thy creatures kneel before Thee,
And in ecstasies of timid love
Delightedly adore Thee.

Hail choicest mystery of God!
Hail wondrous Generation!
The Father's self-sufficient rest!
The Spirit's jubilation!

Dear Person! Dear beyond all words,
Glorious beyond all telling!
Oh with what songs of silent love
Our ravished hearts are swelling!

The Seeming Audacity of His Plan

H. P. Liddon

If it were any merely human plan, we should call it audacity. This audacity is observable, first of all, in the fact that the plan is originally proposed to the world with what might appear to us to be such hazardous completeness. The idea of the kingdom of God issues fully developed from the thought of Christ. Put together the Sermon on the Mount, the Charge to the Twelve Apostles, the Parables of the Kingdom, the Discourse in the Supper-room, and the institution of the Lord's Supper, and the plan of our Saviour is before you, enunciated with an accent of calm, unfaltering conviction that it will be realized in human history.

This is a phenomenon which we can only appreciate by contrasting it with the law to which it is an exception. Generally speaking, an ambitious idea appears at first as a mere outline, and it challenges attention in a tentative way. It is put forward inquiringly, timidly, that it may be completed by the suggestions of friends or modified by the criticism of opponents. The highest genius knows with what difficulty a promising project is launched safely out of the domain of abstract speculation into the region of practical human life.

Social reformers tell us despondingly that facts make sad havoc of their fairest theories, and that schemes which were designed to brighten and to beautify the life of nations are either forgotten altogether, or, like the *Republic* of Plato, are remembered only as famous samples of the impracticable. For whenever a great idea affecting the well-being of society is permitted to force its way into the world of facts, it is liable to be thrust hither and thither, to be compressed, exaggerated, disfigured, mutilated, caricatured. In the first French Revolution some of the most humane sociological projects were distorted into becoming the very animating principles of extraordinary barbarities. In England we are fond of repeating the political maxim that "constitutions are not made, but grow."

Now Jesus Christ our Lord was in the true and very highest sense of the term a social reformer; yet He fully proclaimed the whole of His social plan before He began to realize it. Had He been merely a "great Man" He would have been more prudent. He would have conditioned His design; He would have tested it; He would have developed it gradually; He would have made trial of its working power, and then He would have refashioned it before finally proposing it to the consideration of the world. But His actual course must have seemed one of utter and reckless folly unless the event had shown it to be the dictate of a more than human wisdom.

He speaks as One who is sure of the faultlessness of His design; He is certain that no human obstacle can balk its realization. He produces it simply without effort, without reserve, without exaggeration. He is calm because He is in possession of the future, and sees His way clearly through its tangled maze. There is no intimation of need for change or modification of His plan. He did not, for instance, first aim at a political success and then cover His failure by giving a religious turn or interpretation to His previous manifestoes; He did not begin as a religious teacher and afterwards aspire to convert His increasing religious influence into political capital.

He develops with majestic assurance, with decisive rapidity, the integral features of His work; His teaching centers more and more upon Himself as its central subject, but He nowhere retracts, or modifies, or speaks or acts as would one who feels that he is dependent upon events or agencies which he cannot control.

A poor woman pays Him respect at a feast, and He simply announces that the act will be told as a memorial of her throughout the world (Mt. 26:13); He bids His apostles do all things whatever He had commanded them; He promises them His Spirit as a guide into all necessary truth, but He invests them with no such discretionary powers as might imply that His design would need revision under other circumstances, or could be capable of improvement. He calmly turns the glance of His thought on the long and checkered future which lies clearly displayed before Him, in the immediate foreground of which is His own humiliating death. He speaks as One

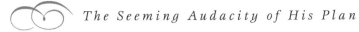

who sees beyond the most distant possibilities, and who knows full well that His work is indestructible. *"The gates of hell,"* He calmly observes, *"shall not prevail against it"* (Mt. 16:18); *"Heaven and earth shall pass away, but My words shall not pass away"*(Mt. 24:35).

But has the plan of Jesus Christ been carried out? The Church of Christ is a living answer to that question. Glance for a moment at the history of the Christian Church from the days of the apostles until now. What is it but a history of gradual, unceasing self-expansion. Compare the Church which sought refuge and which prayed in the upper chamber at Jerusalem with the Church of which Paul is the pioneer and champion in the latter portion of the Acts of the Apostles, or with the Church to which he refers, as already making its way throughout the world in his apostolic epistles.

But you will say, this representation of the history of the Church may suffice for an ideal picture, but it is not history. Is not the verdict of history a different and a less encouraging one? First of all, do Church annals present this spectacle of an ever-widening extension? What is to be said of the spread of great and vital heresies? Of divisions in the Church? Of the rising tide of Islam? Of rationalism and atheism firmly rooted in lands once dominated by the gospel?

We Christians know full well what we have to expect from the human heart in its natural state; while on the other hand we have been told that the gates of hell shall not prevail against the Church of the Redeemer. But, in speculating on the future destinies of the Church, this hopeful confidence of a sound faith may be seconded by the calm estimate of the reflective reason.

Modern unbelief may be deemed less formidable when we steadily observe its moral impotence for all constructive purposes. Its strength and genius lie only in the direction of destruction. It has shown no sort of power to build up any spiritual fabric or system which, as a shelter and a discipline for the hearts and lives of men, can take the place of that which it seeks to destroy. Leaving some of the deepest, most legitimate, and most ineradicable needs of the human soul utterly unsatisfied, modern unbelief can never really hope to permanently establish a popular "religion of humanity."

For this reason modern unbelief, although formidable, will not be deemed so full of menace to the future of the kingdom of our Lord as may sometimes be apprehended by the nervous timidity of Christian piety.

This will appear more certain if from considering the extent of Christ's realm we turn to the intensive side of His work among men. For indeed the depth of our Lord's work in the soul of man has always been more wonderful than its breadth. The moral intensity of the life of a sincere Christian is a more signal illustration of the reality of the reign of Christ, and of the success of His plan, than is the territorial range of any Christian empire. *"The King's daughter is all glorious within."* It is this hidden work that tells the true story.

Christianity may have conferred a new sanction upon civil and domestic relationships among men, and it certainly infused a new life into the most degraded society that the world has yet seen. Still this was not its primary aim; its primary efforts were directed not to this world, but to the next. How complete at this moment is the reign of Christ in the soul of a sincere Christian! Christ is not a limited ruler; He is emphatically an absolute Monarch. Yet His rule is welcomed by His subjects. High above the claims of human teachers the tremendous self-assertion of Jesus Christ echoes on from age to age: *"I am the Truth."* And from age to age the Christian mind responds by a life-long endeavor to bring *"into captivity every thought to the obedience of Christ"* (2 Cor. 10:5). But if Jesus Christ is Lord of the Christian's thought, He is also Lord of the Christian's affections.

Beauty provokes love, and Christ is the highest moral beauty. He does not merely rank as an exponent of the purest morality. He is absolute virtue embodied in a human life, and vividly, energetically set forth before our eyes in the story of the Gospels. As such, He claims to reign over the inmost affections of men. As such, He secures the first place in the heart of every true Christian. To have taken the measure of His beauty and yet not to love Him is, in a Christian's judgment, to be self-condemned. *"If any man love not the Lord Jesus Christ, let him be Anathema Maranatha."*

Ruling the affections of the Christian, Christ is also Master of the Christian will. When He has tamed its native stubbornness He teaches it day by day a more and more pliant accuracy of movement in obedience to Himself. In fact, He is not merely its rule of action but its very motive power; each act of devotion and self-sacrifice of which it is capable is but an extension of the energy of Christ's own moral life. *"Without Me,"* He says to His servants, *"ye can do nothing"* (Jn. 15:5); and with Paul His servants reply, *"I can do all things through Christ which strengtheneth me"* (Phil. 4:13).

This may be expressed in other terms by saying that, both intellectually and morally, Christ is Christianity. Detach Christianity from Christ and it vanishes before your eyes into intellectual vapor. For it is of the essence of Christianity that, hour by hour, the Christian should live in conscious, felt, sustained relationship to the ever-living Author of his creed and life. Christianity is non-existent apart from Christ ; it centers in Christ ; it radiates, now as at the first, from Christ. He is indissolubly associated with every movement of the Christian's deepest life. *"I live,"* exclaims the Apostle, *"yet not I, but Christ liveth in me"* (Gal. 2:20).

The time approaches when it will be seen that the purposes of Christ have triumphed. Then in that day the whole universe shall see that the plan He revealed when He appeared to be a common laborer from Nazareth was in fact the plan of God Himself. And in that day *"...at the name of Jesus every knee [shall] bow, of things in heaven, and things in earth, and things under the earth; and...every tongue [shall] confess that Jesus Christ is Lord, to the glory of God the Father"* (Phil. 2:10-11).

Evening Musing

Author Unknown

Tell me about the Master!
I am weary and worn tonight.
The day lies behind me in shadow,
And only the evening is light.
Light with a radiant glory
That lingers about the west,
My poor heart is aweary, aweary,
And longs like a child for rest.

Tell me about the Master!
Of the wrong He freely forgave,
Of His love and tender compassion,
Of His love that is mighty to save.
For my heart is aweary, aweary,
Of the woes and temptations of life,
Of the error that stalks in the noonday,
Of falsehoods and malice and strife.

Yet, I know that whatever of sorrow,
Or pain or temptation befall,
The Infinite Master hath suffered,
And knoweth and pitieth all.
So tell me the old, old story
That falls on each wound like a balm,
And my heart that was burdened and broken
Shall grow patient, and strong, and calm.

The Face of Christ

John Macbeath

G reat ideas are best comprehended when expressed in simple, accessible things. Beauty is an abstraction until it finds expression in a flower. Music is a fantasy until the notes of an instrument give it speech. Art is ethereal until it embodies itself in sculpture or in picture. The great things of created and uncreated thought are only grasped when they find expression in some easy, intelligible, and often substantial form.

Can we discover any suitable form of expression to embody the glory of God? In the old dispensation men were impressed by magnitude. They felt the awe of the vast reaches of unpeopled space. The magnificence of the heavens, the majesty of the mountains, the mystery of the sea provoked solemn thought and haunting fear. When men looked for indications and evidences of Deity they confessed, *"The heavens declare the glory of God, and the firmament showeth His handiwork"* (Ps. 19:1). The divine glory was revealed in the ample sweep of earth and sky, the immensity of unmeasured space, the golden beams of sunshine, the silver rays of moonlight, the blue heavens studded with twinkling starlight, veiled by morning mist, or marked by the track of fleecy clouds. So regularly do the heavenly bodies move in their silent circles that men measure time by their movements, and sailors steer by their positions. They come and go at their appointed seasons, *"not one faileth."* All these things showed forth the greatness and excellence of the divine handiwork.

The sweet singers of Israel saw God in everything. The clouds were His chariot—He *"walketh upon the wings of the wind."* When the storm rushes through the forest, it is His voice that *"breaketh the cedars."* The joy of harvest awakens fresh gratitude; it is His *"crowning of the year."* To them the earth was crammed with heaven, and every common bush afire with God. "Study nature," urged Kingsley, "do not study nature for its own sake, but as the countenance of God. Try to extract every line of beauty, every association, every moral reflection, every inexpressible feeling from it. Adore God!"

It would be impossible for us to tell how much of the merit we find in nature is to be attributed to the knowledge of life and of God which we have derived from Jesus Christ. An honest investigation would prove that apart from the teaching of Christ and His influence on human thought, we should find nature to be a very inadequate instructor. Nature, without Christ, does not offer intelligent and intimate communion with the Unseen. No one can say that he is acquainted with an artist because he admires the artist's workmanship. The man behind the art must become a voice we hear, a face we recognize; he must make us feel the warmth of human intimacy if we are to have the ennobling sense of kinship.

And so, while the heavens declare the glory of God, the revelation they impart is imperfect and inadequate for the needs of life. Our admiration of the heavens and our appreciation of nature will not teach us lessons of prayer and sacrifice, or wash out the defiling stains of wrong. The power and skill of God may be revealed in nature, but the character of God is revealed in Jesus Christ.

In Christ, the glory of God became personal. It was expressed in terms of love and speech. It came close up to the lives of men, warm, sweet, and tender—lifting them to itself in affection, purity, and peace. *"No man hath seen God at any time; the only begotten Son, which is in the bosom of the Father, He hath declared Him"* (Jn. 1:18). That is the perfect, permanent, final revelation. The glory was revealed in personal form; in living, throbbing personality. That personality was so complete and perfect that Jesus could say with all the calm dignity of truth, *"He that hath seen Me hath seen the Father."*

The glory of condescending grace is manifest in Christ. But the wonder of the advent was that Jesus did not come in clouds of glory, did not come like a king, with scepter and crown and magnificent attendance. He emptied Himself and came in the form of a servant. His world was the street and His retinue was gathered from the poor.

The glory of God shone in the manner of His life. At the very opening of His public ministry we find Him at a wedding feast where He reveals His power to change things. The historical sentence runs, *"This beginning of miracles did Jesus in Cana of Galilee and manifested forth His glory"* (Jn. 2:11). The glory found a new point of expression. It would be a mistake to confine the manifestation of glory to the miracle. The glory shone all over His life and all around the common incidents of experience.

The glory of God in the face of Jesus Christ did not express itself in isolated splendor, in unfamiliar solitariness, in abstinence from social joys. The man who preserves silence may easily be accounted wise. The man who holds himself aloof from the common contact and jostle of life may wrap about him a mysterious veil of sanctity and receive the honor of a saint. But Jesus did not cultivate this habit of holiness. He entered into all the familiar relationships of life in their everyday dress, their easy terms of intimacy, their unaffected simplicity. He mixed with the common crowd of men and things, claiming no exemption from the hardships of life, seeking no shelter from its rough exposure, unprotected from the pride and greatness of the world; and not only did He carry Himself through it all uncorrupted and unspoiled, but He shed everywhere around our common life the hallowing, sanctifying glory of God, and made men feel the greatness of existence when God is in it.

His death and His resurrection are further expressions of the glory of God. They reveal the glory of pardoning mercy and forgiving love, the glory of a great sacrifice, and of complete redemption; the glory of perfected immortality. Jesus was a priest to mankind of the glory of God, which we see not only with His eyes, but in His eyes, and in His face, and in His character. In Him the unseen became visible, the silence found speech, the unknown lived and walked with men. A whole world of progress lies between these two points of expression, *"The heavens declare the glory of God,"* and *"The glory of God in the face of Jesus Christ."* The one indicates greatness, the other expresses grace. The first exhibits power, the second presents personality. The former is material, the latter is spiritual.

The glory of God in the face of Jesus Christ reveals a community of nature between God and men. In the beginning God made man in His own image—so close is grandeur to our dust, so near is God to man, such kinship has man with God. Before the beginning of the

Christian era, profound minds like Plato felt that man was made by nature to be intimate with God. But Jesus revealed a move from the other side. He expressed God's great desire to be intimate with man, to enter into the life of man and transform his world from within.

God is, therefore, not a spectator of this world's tragedy, an unconcerned observer of its woe and want and warfare, as Byron implied, or an indifferent idler, as Carlyle suggested. There is no remoteness in God. He enjoys the world down to the last rose of summer or the last swallow in flight, and above all He loves man. The Old Testament celebrates the glory of creation when the morning stars sang together and all the sons of God shouted for joy. The New Testament heralds the glory of God's redemption, *"There is joy in the presence of the angels of God over one sinner that repenteth."* That is the music of an infinitely mightier and sweeter song.

The glory of God in the face of Jesus Christ is the glory of His entrance into our nature, His revelation of the potentialities of human life. It is the redemption and dedication of our nature that God can express Himself in our flesh. And that expression is not the weakness of God—it is the glory of God. It is the greatest thing God can do. It reveals the greatest thing man can be. What God did in Jesus He seeks to do in you and me. He is not far from us either in distance or in affection. Speech with Him is not a telephonic message across leagues of space. It is a conversation in a closet with the door shut. Fellowship with Him requires no mediating priesthood. God lives and walks with the man himself whose spirit is humble and whose life is surrendered.

That is what Paul is working out when he says, *"We have this treasure in earthen vessels, that the excellency of the power may be of God and not of us"* (2 Cor. 4:7). The vessel is of earth, but through it, as through the simplest transparency, God sheds forth His own exceeding glory. When F. W. H. Myers heard Bishop Temple preach, he felt, as he says, that God was about,

> *For as he spake I knew that God was near,*
> *Reflecting still the immemorial plan;*
> *And, once in Jewry, and for ever here,*
> *Loves as He loved, and ends what He began.*

It is a great thing to know someone whose life illustrates some great principle or expresses some great idea. There are truths we never realize until they are pointed out to us by the high merit of some true life. There are virtues that escape our attention until they are revealed in their scope and variety by someone whose conduct and example exhibit them before our eyes. The service we need is the presence among us of souls that make God real and near. It is by the transfigured lives of His people that God desires to make faith in Him easy to other men. The kingdom is to win its way by the moral superiority of its citizens. The Church is to lighten the world by the glory that radiates through her people. They are the lamps that burn with holy fire. Their kindly light leads wayward feet to God, and men rise up and bless their saving radiance.

There are faces about us that represent ambition, passion, or pride. "Your face, my thane, is as a book where men may read strange matters," said Shakespeare's tragic queen to her husband. There are faces that express avarice, prejudice, guilt, vanity, indulgence; and faces that own an inward faith and loyalty, conscience and courage. Here, face values are life values. The outward and the inward life wear one look, speak with one voice, are one unified whole.

The highest dedication of any life is to interpret and express and illustrate God. The glory of God in the face of Jesus Christ reproduces itself in the character of holy men, revealing purpose, sympathy, strength, faithfulness and love. They make other men feel that in their very neighborhood God Himself is near. "What is there in the face of Dante which is absent from the face of Goethe," Fitzgerald asked Tennyson as they considered the marble busts of the two men. "The divine," answered the poet. The presence or absence of God makes the whole difference between the full and the empty life. For the purposes of sacred art Millais looked for the faces of Jews in London to supply the qualities he desired. For the purposes of His glory God makes no special selection of face. Any life will do.

"In thy face," said a dying scholar to the wife whose devotion had made scholarship possible, "In thy face I have seen the eternal."

> *O God of mountains, stars and boundless spaces!*
> *O God of freedom, and of joyous hearts!*

When Thy face looketh forth from all men's faces,
There will be room enough in crowded marts;
Brood Thou around me, and the noise is o'er;
Thy universe, my closet with shut door.

The glory of God in the face of Jesus Christ has reproduced itself through the ages in the face, soul, and character of those who are His disciples. It is the supreme distinction of the gospel that this solemn dedication is within the reach of all God's people. Every single life may be a separate expression of the glory of God. *"But we all, with open face beholding as in a glass the glory of the Lord, are changed into the same image from glory to glory, even as by the Spirit of the Lord"* (2 Cor. 3:18). Trust Him to do His work. Confront the glory night and day. Face it in success or sorrow. Front it in pleasure or in pain. Surrender your life to its sway. If you do this, I humbly affirm by the Word of the Lord, you will be changed into the same image, and the glory of God will kindle another light by which to lead the feet of men through the dark ways of time to the radiant habitations of eternity.

—*The Face of Christ,* (London: Marshall Morgan and Scott, 1935) pp. 8-16.

The Moral Glory of the Lord Jesus

J. G. Bellett (1795-1864)

Blessed! the Jesus whom we know
In love's unwearied paths below,
Track'd by Evangelists when here,
Is He who is ascended there;
And faith still knows Him as the same,
And reads with confidence His name.
God's glory shone in that blest face,
In power, dignity, and grace.

Lord, I desire to trace Thee more
Than e'er mine eye has done before,
Each passage of Thy life to be
A link between my soul and Thee!
For we shall see Thee as Thou wert,
When every utterance of Thine heart,
Through all Thy works of love divine,
Made all our need and sorrow Thine.

And we shall see Thee as Thou art,
And in Thine image bear our part,
In glory Thou, in glory we,
Bright in the heavenly majesty!
No part of Thy dear life below,
But in its fullness I shall know,
Retouched by Thee, regained by me,
In realms of immortality!

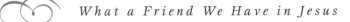

Here changes wrought no change in Thee,
The same from first to last we see;
In life and resurrection, Thou,
Jesus! wert one both then and now.
Yet not in grandeur of the past,
But dearer—what shall ever last—
These were Thy sympathies with us,
And we shall ever know Thee thus.

'Twas joy to Thee, while here on earth,
To hail the bold approach of faith,
The faith that reach'd Thee through the crowd,
Or, though forbidden, cried aloud.
For love delighteth to be used,
Faith's earnest thoughts are ne'er refused:
And this same joy and love in Thee,
We know unchanged eternally.

The look, the sigh, the groan, the tear,
Which marked Thy spirit's pathway here,
We own them still, O Lord, in Thee,
Thy mind, Thy heart, Thy sympathy!
The One who travelled here before,
And tell us we need ask no more,
But stand, with welcome, soon to be
At home for ever, Lord, with Thee!

Thus, memory knows Thee, through the Word,
In all Thy ways and doings, Lord!
'Tis not descriptive words of Thee,
But illustrations clear, we see;
God's glory in Thy face portray'd
Bright, living, likeness without shade.
They who see Thee, the Father see
Wondrous and priceless mystery!

The Fellowship of Tears

L. W. G. Alexander

"*J*esus wept.*"* More wonderful words than these are nowhere to be found in Scripture. The verb translated *"wept"* is unique in its employment here, not found elsewhere. Literally it is, *"Jesus shed tears."* These were tears of sympathy with the bereaved—heaven's gems sparkling on the cheeks of Emmanuel, God with us, revealing to mankind the heart of the Eternal.

The Lord stood by the tomb where a loved and only brother had been laid, and where two brokenhearted sisters mourned him. Could He not have prevented this sorrow? Yes. Could He have not come earlier and robbed death of its triumph? Yes.

But this sorrow was permitted for the glory of God. In one sense the words of the sisters were true: "Lord, if Thou hadst been here my brother had not died!" Death cannot abide His presence. Here, then, we find it clearly taught that God permits death and sorrow to come upon His loved ones that He may be glorified thereby. This is a fact worthy of deep pondering.

Had Lazarus not died these words would never have been written, *"Jesus shed tears."* Had Lazarus not died, these silent witnesses to the anguish that tore the Saviour's heart in view of human loss and sorrow would never have flowed. Had Lazarus not died this special revelation of the heart of God would have never been granted to men to support them in the hour of anguish and sorrow. The death of Lazarus has enriched the race with a vision of God, the glory of which can only be discerned through tear-dimmed eyes.

These sisters had seen the Lord Jesus often. They had ministered to His wants. They had listened to His words. They loved to welcome Him to their home and to gaze upon His face. He brought the sunshine of heaven with Him, and diffused its peace around. They

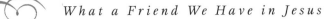

rejoiced with Him, and He rejoiced with them. He touched them in their joy; can He touch them also in their sorrow? They had seen that face radiant with holy joy; they must see it likewise clouded with anguish and behold the teardrops coursing down. Thus would He teach them, and us, how to *"rejoice with them that do rejoice, and weep with them that weep"* (Rom. 12:15).

We reach a common bond in the brotherhood of tears. I weep with my brother at morn; he weeps with me before nightfall. May the tears of the Son of God at the tomb of Lazarus not appeal to our hearts in vain! He has placed a holy dignity upon tears.

The tears of the Lord at this time are all the more wonderful as we contemplate the fact that He knew He was about to raise Lazarus from the dead and restore him to these sisters and thrill their hearts with an unexpected joy. Not for them alone, therefore, were these tears shed. They were shed to assure our hearts that He sees and understands and sympathizes with us.

Of nothing are we better assured from Scripture than that the Lord is still able to enter into the sorrows of His people, as He did during the days of His flesh, to sympathize with them in bereavement, and to send them divine succor from on high. To this very end did He suffer when here below. *"Wherefore in all things it behoved Him to be made like unto His brethren, that He might be a merciful and faithful high priest...."* (Heb. 2:17).

The words of the angels to the disciples after His ascension were: *"This same Jesus..."* (Acts 1:11). He sits upon the throne of God, having been absent in person from our world for more than two thousand years, but these words prove that He is still unchanged, that He abides the *"same Jesus."* True it is that He now is where tears can never flow. But the compassion that caused Him to shed tears in the days of His flesh remains unchanged, and by the Spirit He draws near to assure our hearts of His divine sympathy.

Our Great High Priest

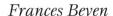

Frances Beven

Sweet to trace His toiling footsteps
Here amidst the desert sands;
Bear in memory all His sorrow,
Thorn-clad head and pierced hands!

Learn His love beside the manger,
Learn it on the stormy wave,
By the well, and in the garden
Learn it by the cross and grave.

Yet not only in remembrance
Do we watch that stream of love
Still a mighty torrent flowing
From the throne of God above.

Still a treasure all uncounted
Still a story half untold
Unexhausted and unfathomed,
Fresh as in the days of old.

Christ at God's right hand unwearied
By our tale of shame and sin,
Day by day, and hour by hour,
Welcoming each wanderer in.

On His heart amidst the glory,
Bearing all our grief and care;
Every burden, ere we feel it,
Weighed and measured in His prayer.

Fragrant thus with priestly incense
Each distress, each sorrow tells

Thoughts that fill the heart of Jesus
In the glory where He dwells.

All His love, His joy, His glory,
By His Spirit here made known,
While that Spirit speaks the sorrows
Of His saints before the throne.

He, of old the Man of Sorrows,
Pleads before the Father's face,
Knowing all the needed solace,
Claiming all the needed grace.

We, so faithless and so weary,
Serving with impatient will
He unwearied in our service,
Gladly, ministering still.

On the night of His betrayal,
In the glory of the throne,
Still with faithful patience washing
All defilement from His own.

When the Father's house resoundeth
With the music and the song;
When the bride in glorious raiment
Sees the One who loved so long;

Then for new and blessed service
Girt afresh will He appear,
Stand and serve before His angels
Those who waited for Him here.

He who led them through the desert,
Watched and guided day by day,
Turned the flinty rocks to water,
Made them brooks beside the way.

He will bring them where the fountains
Fresh and full spring forth above,
Still throughout the endless ages
Serving in the joy of love.

The Master Key

A. T. Schofield

I have found the Master Key of Heaven that unlocks everything: C.H.R.I.S.T. Yes, I know it is an old story; but, oh, the newness of its wonders!

Recently, I went on a tour for the Lord in the north of England. To me it has been a series of miracles of the love of Christ. Perhaps part of the wonder is that northern English people never seem to display their feelings. But my Master Key unlocked every heart.

Once I rather doubted its power. It was at a morning service, and the faces were as carved out of granite. But I tried my Master Key, and was amazed at its power—the hand-grip, the moist eyes, the smile struggling to the surface, all told that each heart had been opened! At another time, two once-bitter rivals met, and at the close gripped each other's hands for the first time in twelve years.

This Master Key also unlocked to me the untouched unity of God's great family. Everywhere I was with my own people. The idea of differences seemed absurd and profane. We were all so absolutely one in Christ, and that independently of all labels which we didn't even trouble to make clear.

But this marvel not only unlocked all hearts, but all houses from the highest to the lowest—from mansions of ancient splendor to little houses in long rows and small streets, where dear members of the Royal Family lived. The Master Key not only unlocked the door of these, but the best bedrooms, turning sometimes master and mistress out of them, all for the love of an adorable Lord.

It unlocked all purses, too, for nothing was too good for those that came in His dear Name. In two wealthy abodes, I thought it was some old link of friendship that opened the doors; but soon found that the love of Christ was the real mainspring. The widow of one of our merchant princes never failed to come to the squalid, crowded hall and sit on a hard bench to catch something of the fragrance of the Rose of Sharon.

This Master Key unlocked all classes, all races, all ages, all conditions of men, in an absolute Spirit-formed unity. But, oh, the faces! How can I describe the sight night after night when, at a certain point in the address, I used the Master Key! It was just as when the lights are turned on in a hall. The whole sea of faces became radiant with joy. The subject when the sudden change was most visible was "The Lord's parousia." To me it was not the "path of the just" but the faces of the just that were as the light of the dawn; and I could see that all the faces were looking for *"that blessed hope."*

The Master Key also unlocks all love. Having to leave our car in the north for a long all-day journey south, we carefully arranged all our trains to correspond. But it was all in vain, for our second train was cancelled. We didn't know, but God did, and the night before had opened the heart of an entire stranger with this Key. We never thought to see him again, but as we stepped into the first train, he was in the same car! Not only so, but when we found at his destination that our second train was cancelled, he carried our luggage for us; told us of another train from another station that would reach our destination at same time; packed all our things in a taxi and sent it off, and all was well; for the Master Key had opened this stranger's heart, and goodness and mercy had followed us all that day.

Have I said enough of the real, warm family feeling among all sorts and conditions of men never seen before?

Many of the dear homes we entered were adorned with framed texts of Scripture. These always remind me of the old lady in Devonshire, formerly a nurse's aide in a war hospital, to whom a grateful French officer presented a beautifully engraved paper as a memento. She thought so much of it that she framed it and hung it up in her room, till at last a friend saw it and explained it was a French banknote for £400. So she took it down, put her name to it, and cashed it. I sometimes wonder if all these beautiful framed checks that hang on our walls have been signed and cashed by their owners!

O How He Loves!

Marianne Nunn

One there is above all others; O how He loves!
His is love beyond a brother's; O how He loves!
Earthly friends may fail or leave us,
One day soothe, the next day grieve us,
But this Friend will ne'er deceive us;
O how He loves!

'Tis eternal life to know Him; O how He loves!
Think, O think how much we owe Him; O how He loves!
With His precious blood He bought us,
In the wilderness He sought us,
To His fold securely brought us,
O how He loves!

We have found a friend in Jesus; O how He loves!
'Tis His great delight to bless us; O how He loves!
How our hearts delight to hear Him,
Bid us dwell in safety near Him,
Why should we distrust or fear Him?
O how He loves!

Through His name we are forgiven; O how He loves!
Backward shall our foes be driven; O how He loves!
Best of blessings He'll provide us,
Nought but good shall e'er betide us,
Safe to glory He will guide us,
O how He loves!

The Only Face She Could See

H. A. Ironside

The story is told of one of the generals of Cyrus the Great, king of Persia. He came home from a campaign and was shocked to find that in his absence his wife had been arrested and was languishing in prison, charged with treachery against her country. Her trial was to be held that very day. The general hastened to the court of Cyrus, and the guards brought in his own beloved wife.

She, poor woman, pale and anxious, tried to answer the charges brought against her, but all to no avail. Her husband, standing near, heard the stern voice of the Persian ruler pronounce the death sentence. As they were about to drag her away to behead her, he ran forward and threw himself down at the feet of the Emperor.

"Oh, sire," he cried, "not she, but me. Let me give my life for hers. Put me to death, but spare my wife."

As Cyrus looked upon him, he was so touched by his deep devotion to his wife that his heart was softened. He remembered, too, how faithful this servant had been, and he gave the command that the wife should go free. She was fully pardoned.

As her husband led her out of the room, he said to her, "Did you notice the kind look in the eyes of the Emperor as he pronounced the word of pardon?"

"I did not see the face of the Emperor," she said. "The only face that I could see was that of the man who was willing to die for me."

Oh, when we get Home, when we see the face of the Man who did die for us, how our hearts will praise Him! How we will rejoice in His presence as we say, *"The Son of God...loved me, and, gave Himself for me"* (Gal. 2:20).

Jesus Only

Frances Ridley Havergal

"Jesus only," midst the shadows,
That within the valley lie;
He it is who calls us onward,
To the glory of the sky.

'Tis His pierced hand points upward,
Far above the mountain's height,
Far above the valley shadows,
To the radiant glory light.

"Jesus only" when in trouble,
When our heart is full of grief,
He alone can give us comfort,
He alone can bring relief.

He alone knows all the heart-pangs
He can fully sympathize;
And His arms are thrown around us,
While He wipes our weeping eyes.

"Jesus only" on life's ocean,
When the billows wildly roar;
He it is who holds the helm,
Guides us to the golden shore.

He alone is our sure refuge,
Speaking words of loving cheer,
Bids us when the storm roars loudest,
Just to trust and not to fear.

"Jesus only" when the sunbeams
Gleam around our pilgrim way;
When no shadows seem to darken,
Throughout all the long bright day:

Then He comes and walks beside us,
Whispering words of tend'rest love;
Tells us of the light and glory,
In the sunny land above.

"Jesus only" at that moment
When He comes to claim His own;
These eyes then shall gaze in rapture,
On His face, and His alone.

"Jesus only" in those mansions,
Which He's now gone to prepare,
It will still be "Jesus only,"
'Mid the myriad throngs up there.

The Perfect Man

C. H. Mackintosh

The Lord Jesus was the only perfect Man this world has ever seen. He was all and always perfect, under the eye of God and before men—perfect in thought, perfect in word, and perfect in action. In Him every moral quality met, and this in perfect proportion and manifestation. No single feature predominated. In *"the Man Christ Jesus"* there were perfectly blended a majesty which overawed, and a gentleness which gave perfect ease in His presence. The scribes and Pharisees met His withering rebukes, while the poor Samaritan, and *"the woman that was a sinner,"* found themselves unaccountably yet irresistibly attracted to Him.

No one feature in His character displaced another, for all was in fair and comely proportion. He could say in reference to the 5000 hungry people that followed Him in the barren desert, *"Give ye them to eat,"* and when they were filled, He commanded, *"Gather up the fragments that remain, that nothing be lost."* The benevolence and the economy are seen to be equally perfect, and neither interferes with the other. Each shines in its own proper sphere.

He could not send away a hungry people unfed, nor could He suffer a fragment of God's supply to be wasted. He would bountifully meet the need of men with a full and liberal hand, and when that was done, He would see to every atom of that which was not required, so that nothing provided by God for human need should be lost. The selfsame hand that was widely opened to every form of human need was firmly closed against all prodigality and waste. There was nothing cheap in His measure of supply, nor was there any extravagance in the manner of His providing for man's need. In this, as in all else in which the Lord Jesus appears, He is ever absolutely perfect in His character and ways.

What a lesson there is in all this to us! How frequently with us does benevolence resolve itself into unwarrantable waste, while on the other hand how often is our economy marred by the exhibition of a miserly spirit. At times our selfish hearts refuse to open themselves to supply the needs that present themselves, while at other times we squander, through a wanton extravagance, that which might meet the need of many a fellow-creature.

But there were none of these inequalities in our blessed Lord. He was perfect in all He did and gave, and equally so in what He refused to sanction. How blessed and refreshing to the soul it is to be so occupied with Him in all the perfections of His character and ways as manifested throughout His earthly course.

Creation's light was sweet indeed,
But soon it changed to gloom,
When sin obtained a footing there,
And man received his doom.

The light that from the Saviour shone
Was perfect in its beam,
And gave to all on whom it fell
A glorious heavenly gleam.

'Tis this that gladdens holy heaven:
No other light is there;
The glory of the Lamb alone
Illumes the city fair.

An artist drew a picture of a wintry twilight—the trees heavily laden with snow, and a dreary, dark house, lonely and desolate in the midst of the storm. It was a sad picture. Then, with a quick stroke of yellow, he put a light in one window. The effect was magnificent. The entire scene was transformed into a vision of comfort and cheer. The coming of Christ was just such a light in a dark world.

The Man Divine

Frances Beven

In the Paradise of glory
Is the Man divine;
There my heart, O God, is tasting
Fellowship with Thine;
Called to share Thy joy unmeasured,
Now in heaven begun;
I rejoice with Thee, O Father,
In Thy glorious Son.

Round me is creation groaning,
Death, and sin, and care;
But there is a rest remaining,
And my Lord is there.
There I find a blessed stillness
In His courts of love;
All below but strife and darkness,
Cloudless peace above.

'Tis a solitary pathway
To that fair retreat—
Where in deep and sweet communion
Sit I at His feet.
In that glorious isolation,
Loneliness how blest,
From the windy storm and tempest
Have I found my rest.

The Neglected Parable

F. W. Boreham

Here is the neglected parable—the Cinderella of the parables! A million sermons have been preached on the parable of the Ten Virgins, the Prodigal Son, and all the rest. But here is Christ's crowning parable, a masterpiece of imagery that He left to the last, and only unfolded from the throne of His glory.

"I am Alpha and Omega," He said repeatedly (Rev. 1:8, 11; 21:6; 22:13). And since Alpha is simply the first letter in the Greek alphabet, and Omega the last, it is as if He said, "I am the A and the Z. I am the Alphabet!" It is an arresting simile, and worthy of the closest scrutiny; yet strange to say, we seldom pay it the slightest attention. It is pleasant to reflect that He, who loved all common and familiar things, sparrows and ravens, lilies and wheat, took the commonplace letters that little children have to learn, and transmuted them into an exquisite symbol of His redemptive glory.

The alphabet rises to sudden splendor when the risen and ascended Saviour enlists it in His program of self-revelation. Long, long ago, a startled shepherd was commanded to address a nation and a throne in the Name of the Most High. He asked for the credentials by which he might sustain so august a commission. *"Say,"* he was bidden, *"say that I AM hath sent thee!"*

"I Am—!"

"I Am—who? I Am—what?"

For centuries that question stood unanswered, that sentence remained incomplete. It was a magnificent fragment. It stood like a monument that the sculptor had never lived to finish; like a poem that the composer, dying with all his music in him, had left with its closing stanzas unsung. But the Sculptor of that statue was not dead; the Singer of that song had not perished. For, behold, He liveth for evermore! And in the fullness of time, He reappeared and filled in the gap that had so long stood blank.

> "I Am—!"
> "I Am—what? I Am—who?"
> *"I am—the Bread of Life!"*
> *"I am—the Light of the World!"*
> *"I am—the Door!"*
> *"I am—the True Vine!"*
> *"I am—the Good Shepherd!"*
> *"I am—the Way, the Truth and the Life!"*
> *"I am—the Resurrection and the Life!"*

And thus, verse by verse, He worked His way to the sublime climax of that closing stanza: *"I am Alpha and Omega!"* "I am—A and Z!" "I am—the Alphabet." The art of symbolism can rise to no loftier altitude than that. What, I wonder, can such symbolism portray?

The Inexhaustible Christ

"I am the Alphabet!" I have sometimes stood in one of our great public libraries. I have surveyed with astonishment the serried ranks of English literature. I have looked up, tier above tier, gallery above gallery, shelf above shelf, the books climbed to the very roof, while looking before me and behind me, they stretched as far as I could see. And what do all these tons of tomes contain? They contain simply the 26 letters of the alphabet, arranged in kaleidoscopic variety. Each poet and novelist juggled with the letters, shuffled them, and marshalled them in an order that they had never before assumed; but each drew only upon those 26 letters for every line that he penned.

Have all these hundreds of thousands of writers, penning these millions upon millions of books, begun to exhaust the alphabet? Not a bit of it! The writers of tomorrow will find the alphabet as fresh, as unworn, and as ready to do their purpose as did the writers of yesterday and yesteryear.

"I am—the Alphabet!" The Saviour means that, in His redemptive fullness and splendor, He is absolutely incapable of exhaustion. The ages may draw upon His grace; the men of all nations and kindreds and peoples and tongues, a multitude that no man can number. A host that no statistician can count may kneel in contrition at His feet, availing themselves of His pity and pardon and peace, but they are drinking of a fountain that can never run dry. Like the alphabet, He is inexhaustible.

> *His love is as great as His power,*
> *And knows neither measure nor end.*

THE INDISPENSABILITY OF CHRIST

Literature, with all its hoarded treasure, is as inaccessible as diamonds on the moon until I have mastered the alphabet. I may wander through the most gigantic and glorious libraries, with all the wealth of poetry and history and science and travel and philosophy and romance ranged in bewildering luxuriance around me; but unless I first become acquainted with Him, I can enjoy neither the choicest treasures of this life nor the radiant raptures of the life to come. I must know the Lord Jesus Christ, the Key to Life!

As the disciples discovered on the road to Emmaus, I cannot understand my Bible unless I take Him as the Key to it all. I cannot understand the processes of historical development until I have accorded Him the central place in the pageant of the ages. I cannot anticipate with equanimity the august unfoldings of the days to come until I have seen the keys of the eternities swinging at His girdle. At every point, Christ is life's supreme indispensability.

THE INVINCIBILITY OF CHRIST

He is at the beginning, that is to say, and He goes right through to the very end. There is nothing in the alphabet before A; there is nothing after Z. However remote the period at which your interpretation of the universe places the beginning of things, you will find Him there. When things first began, it was because He began them. When the drama ends, it will be because He brings down the curtain. And all the way through, He is marshalling the pageant of the aeons. He is everlastingly in command. The story of the ages may be told in a sentence: "Christ first, Christ last, and nothing between but Christ." Having begun, He completes. He goes right through!

THE ADAPTABILITY OF CHRIST

Nothing on the face of the earth is as adaptable as the alphabet. No two of us are alike, yet we can each express our individualities through the agency of the alphabet. In whatever mood I find myself, I can set pen to paper and express that mood exactly. The alphabet is the most fluid, the most accommodating, the most plastic device known to men. The lover takes these 26 letters and makes them the vehicle for the expression of his passion; the poet transforms them into a song that shall be sung for centuries; the judge turns them into a sentence that sends a shuddering wretch to a felon's cell and a hangman's rope. What could be more adaptable than this?

And just because of this remarkable quality in the alphabet, Jesus employs it as an emblem of Himself. He adapts Himself, with divine exactitude, to the individual needs of each of us.

I do not need Him in the precise sense in which Paul needed Him, or Bunyan, or Wesley, or Spurgeon. But I need Him in a way of my own, and He can match that peculiar need of mine as the alphabet can lend itself to each separate man and mood. To each individual, the spiritual experiences of others sound unconvincing. Their case is not my case. I may not have sinned more than others, but I have sinned differently. *"We have turned every one to his own way."*

The narratives of other pilgrims do not quite reflect my condition. But the beauty of it is that, like the alphabet, Christ adapts Himself with the most perfect precision to my own peculiar and desperate need. Until we have discovered the amazing facility with which Jesus can meet our distinctive yearnings and needs, we cannot possibly appreciate the power and value of the cross.

Alpha and Omega

Aurelius Prudentius, 413

Of the Father's love begotten
Ere the worlds began to be,
He is Alpha and Omega,
He the Source, the Ending He,
Of the things that are, that have been,
And that future years shall see
Evermore and evermore.

Oh, that birth forever blessed
When the Virgin, full of grace,
By the Holy Ghost conceiving,
Bare the Saviour of our race,
And the Babe, the world's Redeemer,
First revealed His sacred face.

O ye heights of heaven, adore Him;
Angel hosts, His praises sing;
Powers, dominions, bow before Him
And extol our God and King.
Let no tongue on earth be silent,
Every voice in concert ring.

Christ, to Thee, with God the Father,
And, O Holy Ghost, to Thee
Hymn and chant and high thanksgiving
And unending praises be,
Honor, glory, and dominion,
And eternal victory
Evermore and evermore.

The Supremacy of Christ

W. Fraser Naismith

What an elixir for the soul is provided in the contemplation of the greatness and glories of our Lord Jesus Christ! God has declared that He *"gave Him to be the head over **all things**."* He has also decreed that *"He might fill **all things**."* Here are three statements which allude to Christ's transcendental greatness.

The preacher in Ecclesiastes 5:8 refers to One who is *"higher than the highest."* The writer to the Hebrews (7:26) referring to our great High Priest, states that He is *"higher than the heavens."* And in Psalm 89:27, God says, *"I will make Him My firstborn, higher than the kings of the earth."*

The Book of Ecclesiastes is the place into which we may enter and listen awhile to the preacher. In his dissertation, he discloses how carefully he has tested everything under the sun in an endeavor to discover something from which true happiness might be procured. The summation of all his research can best be told in his own words: *"All is vanity and vexation of spirit."*

Had real, true and lasting joy been discovered in the realms of the ephemeral, then we might have said there was no need for Abraham to maintain a tent and an altar—things that suggest the transient—and to look for a city which has foundations whose builder and maker is God. Nor would it have been necessary for Moses to suffer affliction with the people of God if Egypt's pleasures were of an enduring nature. This world can provide nothing of a lasting character and its joys are short-lived. It was during these experimental enterprises that the preacher in Ecclesiastes makes reference to One who is *"higher than the highest."* Potentates there were like himself at the time of this treatise, yet no matter how lofty their thrones, he would assure us that there was One who far excelled them all.

Go back in thought to the time when there were no men upon this earth. Heaven's hierarchy (creatures of His hand destined to serve Him day and night forever) were onlookers at the laying of earth's foundations, when they emitted that jubilant sound, blending their voices in holy unison in that prehistoric song. It was by their disposition that Israel received the law; and by whose instrumentality the elect on the earth shall be gathered out of the kingdom. As servants of God, they were ever responsive to His commands and executed His holy will. Such creatures can only be faintly considered by us, nor can we apprehend their greatness and dignity, yet, no matter how great or dignified they may be, they are creatures of His hand, and He is their great Creator, higher than the highest!

Cherubim and seraphim may be justly considered as being associated with the intrinsic holiness of God and supporting every edict that emanates from the throne of His holiness. "Lofty creatures," you say; but they are only creatures. He is their Creator and therefore He is higher than the highest.

Bring into relief the mighty men of faith, whose names are inscribed in the annals of eternal renown for their illustrious deeds, whether they be patriarchs, priests, prophets or princes—each has lived and exercised authority by the authority of Another, that is God's Son. No matter what the particular characteristic may be—walking with God; pleasing God; believing and obeying God—each was a creature of *His* hand, who, when He takes His place in creation is *"firstborn of all creation,"* and this suggests to us priority of rank and dignity of position, not point of time.

It matters not what dignity is conferred upon angels or men, there is One who holds that supreme position in glorious headship, to whom every knee must bow in the acknowledgment of His supremacy, who leaves the stamp of glory on every subordinate authority. Throughout all time and eternity One has eclipsed all others. He, who took the lowest place, is altogether *"higher than the highest."*

Immanuel's Land

Anne Ross Cousin (1824-1906)

The sands of time are sinking,
The dawn of heaven breaks,
The summer morn I've sighed for—
The fair, sweet morn awakes.
Dark, dark hath been the midnight,
But day-spring is at hand,
And glory—glory dwelleth
In Immanuel's land.

There the Red Rose of Sharon
Unfolds its heartsome bloom,
And fills the air of heaven
With ravishing perfume.
Oh! to behold its blossom,
While by its fragrance fanned,
Where glory—glory dwelleth
In Immanuel's land.

The King there in His beauty
Without a veil is seen;
It were a well-spent journey,
Though seven deaths lay between.
The Lamb, with His fair army,
Doth on Mount Zion stand,
And glory—glory dwelleth
In Immanuel's land.

Oh, Christ, He is the fountain—
The deep, sweet well of love!
The streams on earth I've tasted,
More deep I'll drink above.
There, to an ocean fullness,
His mercy doth expand,
And glory—glory dwelleth
In Immanuel's land.

Here flowers need night's cool darkness,
The moonlight and the dew.
So Christ's, from one who loved it,
His shining oft withdrew;
And then for cause of absence,
My troubled soul I scann'd—
But glory shadeless shineth
In Immanuel's land.

Soon shall the cup of glory
Wash down earth's bitterest woes,
Soon shall the desert briar
Break into Eden's rose;
The curse shall change to blessing—
The name on earth that's banned
Be graven on the white stone
In Immanuel's land.

Oh, I am my Beloved's
And my Beloved is mine!
He brings a poor vile sinner
Into His "house of wine."
I stand upon His merit,
I know no other stand,
Not e'en where glory dwelleth,
In Immanuel's land.

Letters of Comfort

From the correspondence of Viscountess Powerscourt

Oh! that our hearts were always bubbling up, boiling with this matter, like wine that hath no vent, ready to burst its bottles, constrained to speak about our King. Oh! that He so dwelt in our hearts by faith that out of their abundance our speech might be as spikenard sending forth its pleasant smell, ointment pouring forth His name, that this good treasure, this mine of wealth, might be continually emptying itself in consolations into our own bosoms, and enriching all around.

But who is this King that we should leave all other subjects to speak of Him? The Lord strong and mighty, the Lord mighty in our battles, the Lord of hosts, the King of glory. My Lord, who sits at the Lord's right hand, till every evil in my heart shall become His footstool. The King who, in spite of the heathen raging, the kings of the earth standing up, the rulers taking counsel against Him, shall be set on the holy hill of Sion. A King who has come to His people in a chariot paved with love. A King with many crowns, the most radiant, the most becoming of which is the one He received in the day of His espousals (Song 3:2). A King whose greatest glory is His bride.....betrothed and united to Himself for ever. A King who, in the day of the gladness of His heart, shall stretch forth His hand to you and me, and say in the presence of men, angels, and devils, *"Come, ye blessed of My Father."*

He is a King who has Himself prepared the kingdom, who by the love-tokens He distills on us day after day, who, having prepared a kingdom that will satisfy, is now preparing us for it. By His dispensations and His consolations, He proves He has considered our frame, knows what will satisfy, even to enter into the joy of our Lord, A King who has enriched His Church by His poverty, nourished it by His riches. In a word, Jesus of Nazareth, the King of the Jews. Say, dear friend, have we not volumes to unfold respecting this King?

Why then do we so often spend our time, while in the company of our Father's children, talking on subjects we despise and consider trifles? Is it not because out of the abundance of the heart the mouth speaks? Alas! How grievously have I to accuse myself on this point; in nothing do I feel so dependent; and when I do speak, how many double, treble motives; how often seeking self instead of Jesus, proved by silence before those who dislike it; how often ashamed of Him; how often irritated when opposed; how often playing with the subject; how little feeling what I speak. How humbling; how astonished would you be did you know me. All the love of angels and saints put together, could not have patience with me....He alone could "silent stand, and wait to show His love."

Surely it is no hard demand that is required, only to be loving subjects, and how gracious where He demands this. He does not call on us to love an unknown friend, but with His own pencil has drawn for us the object to be loved.

Two questions are natural when called to give our affections. First, what sort of person is He? Second, what is His mind towards me? Let us hear what answer God has given.

What sort of person? *"Chiefest among ten thousand," "fairer than the children of men," "altogether lovely," "as the apple tree among the trees of the wood;"* not only *"the first-born of every creature,"* but *"the image of the invisible God, the brightness of His glory, the express image of His person;"* even God Himself, who made and upholds all things in heaven and earth. What does Peter say when he was the witness of His majesty? What does John, when he saw Him standing in the midst of the seven golden candlesticks? Every knee bows to His name, every tongue shall confess Him Lord; for He is holy, harmless, undefiled, separate from sinners—this is our King.

But what is His mind towards us? *"Full of grace and truth;"* out of His fullness ever pouring grace upon grace. His words to us are powerful, to overcome by love, a sharp two-edged sword, yet as the sound of many waters, *"most sweet,"* as lilies dropping sweet-smelling myrrh; *"never man spake as He spake,"* gave His enemies testimony: for they *"wondered at the gracious words which proceeded out of His mouth."* This is your Beloved and Friend, as well as King, who has grace poured into His lips on purpose to speak a word in season to the weary; blessed weariness which brings a word from Him!

Sweet to have our Beloved, our King! Comfortable to be able to say, my Jesus reigns. With what confidence we may lay ourselves back in His arms, and say, *"undertake for me."* Blessed to be one with Him whom God has blessed for ever. Blessed to have our salvation and His glory bound up in the same bundle. Blessed to know He has gone through every class in our wilderness-school.

Are you satisfied with this King? For He is your King for ever and ever. May our repose in Him answer the question. Are you contented to have Him, and leaving all others to cleave only to Him? For this Beloved is yours, and you are His. May the devotedness of our affections, lives, and words, answer, *"Lord, Thou knowest all things; Thou knowest that I love Thee."* And, oh! may we be kept from acting as one who is ashamed of his choice.

FROM HER LETTER TO A WIDOW, RECENTLY BEREAVED

Is your happy soul still lifted up, able in His light to walk through darkness? I know the dreary waste that lies before you. How his dear, dear company is missed, how tasteless and insipid everything appears; how you want that affection which entered into every trifle which concerned you, how you want an adviser, a protector, such a companion, one to weep when you weep, to rejoice when you rejoice. I know well what it is to lie down at night and say, "Where is he?", to awake in the morning, and find him gone, to hear the hour strike day after day, at which you once expected his daily return home to his too happy fireside, and find nothing but a remembrance that embitters all the future here.

O my poor, poor friend, if I cannot feel for you, who so often partook of your happiness—sweet, precious time I have been allowed to enjoy with you both, who can? However, it is well that you have another to feel for you. If I know the meaning of the word sorrow, I also know of a joy a stranger intermeddleth not with.

How tenderly our compassionate Lord speaks of the widow! as a parent who feels the punishment more than the chastened child. He seems intent to fill up every gap love has been forced to make: one of His errands from heaven was to bind up the broken-hearted. He has an answer for every complaint you may ever be tempted to make.

Do you say you have none now to follow, to walk with, to lean on? He will follow you, and invite you to come up from the wilderness, leaning on Him as your Beloved. Is it that you want one to be interested in all your concerns? *"Casting all your cares upon Him, for He careth for you."* A protector? *"Let thy widows trust in Me."* An adviser? Wonderful Counselor! Companion? *"I will not leave you comfortless...I will come to you...I will never leave you, nor forsake you...I have not called you servants, but friends...Behold, I stand at the door, and knock; if any man hear My voice, and open the door, I will come in to him, and will sup with him, and he with Me."* One to weep with you? In all their affliction He was afflicted: Jesus wept.

When you lie down, you are safe under the shadow of His wings, under the banner of His love. When you awake, He is still about your path and about your bed. It is worth being afflicted to become intimately acquainted, and to learn to make use of *"the chief of ten thousand...the altogether lovely...the brother born for adversity...the friend that sticketh closer than a brother...the friend of sinners."*

Divine Sympathy

Viscountess Powerscourt (1800-1836)

Jesus, my sorrow lies too deep
For human ministry;
It knows not how to tell itself
To any but to Thee.

Thou dost remember still, amid
The glories of God's throne,
The sorrows of mortality,
For they were once Thine own.

Yes, for as if Thou would'st be God,
E'en in Thy misery,
There's been no sorrow but Thine own
Untouched by sympathy.

Jesus, my fainting spirit brings
Its fearfulness to Thee,
Thine eye at least can penetrate
The clouded mystery.

And is it not enough, enough,
This holy sympathy?
There is no sorrow e'er so deep
But I may bring to Thee.

Written upon the death of her husband, when she was age 23.

The Crowned Christ Reigning

S. D. Gordon

I t's a long lane that has no turning. Every valley leads up a hillside to a top. Every storm ends in sunshine at the last. Every night runs out; the dawn will break, the new day comes; the shadows flee before the new shining. The battle for right will end in victory, a decisive victory. There'll be no draw here. Faith wins at last. It's been a long night of fighting. Sometimes it seems endless.

The man in the thick of the fight, with moist brow and clenched hand and quick breath and throbbing heart sometimes sobs out the prayer, "O Lord, how long before the night is over, and the dawn breaks?" And quietly through the smoke and din of the conflict a still, small voice says, "Steady, My child, steady; the day is surely coming, and with day victory; steady, steady a bit longer."

Revelation 20:4-22 records in vision the time when the fight is over, the victory won. And God's visions always become realities. The vision is yet for the appointed time, and it pants breathlessly toward reality among the nations. Then there will be war no longer, but universal peace.

There is one part of the picture particularly comforting. That vast majority, the poor, will be especially guarded and cared for. There will be no hungry people, nor cold, nor poorly clad; no unemployed begging for a chance to earn a dry crust, and no workers fighting for a fair share of the fruit of their toil. But there are yet tenderer touches on the canvas. Broken hearts will be healed, prison doors unhung, broken family circles complete again.

An issue of *The Sunday School Times* tells a simple, touching incident of a mission hall in Korea. A Korean woman living in the country heard of the wonderful things happening there, and came to town to find out for herself, and get some help. But she didn't know where the hall was, nor what name it was called. So she asked for the place where they cured the broken heart. At once she was directed to the mission hall. That sort of thing will become a blessed common-place in the beginning of the kingdom time.

Then there are certain radical changes in nature. Splendid rivers of waters are to flow through or by Jerusalem, suggesting dramatic changes in the formation of the land there. That fortress city on the hilltop becomes the world's metropolis, a mighty city, with rivers floating a world's commerce. The light of sun and moon will be greatly intensified, so influencing the fertility of the earth. Before their healing light and heat, in the newly tempered atmosphere, all poisonous growths, the blight of drought, and suffering of untem-pered heat, will disappear. With this goes a change in the animal cre-ation. Beasts that are dreaded because of their ferocity and treachery and poisonous power will be wholly changed. There will be mutual cessation of cruelty to animals by man, and of danger to man by ani-mals, for all hate and violence will be gone.

Someone raises his eyebrows skeptically and says, "What fairy tale, what skipper's yarn, is this?" Well, I frankly confess that I don't know anything about this matter, except what I find in this old Book of God. But I confess, too, that I try studiously to get a common sense, poised, Spirit-enlightened understanding of what this Book does tell. Then I accept it, and go by it, regardless of probabilities or improbabilities. It may seem like a fairy tale, yet it is only the full fruition of the kingdom sampled when our Lord was on earth.

As we turn to the Gospel pages, we find the kingdom to be the chief thing Jesus is talking about. The Gospel days are an example of the days of the kingdom in the personal blessings bestowed. Read through these accounts of blind eyes opened, the lame walking, the maimed made whole, the dumb singing, the distressed in whatever way relieved, the ignorant instructed, the sinful wooed, and the bad of heart and life being blessedly changed.

All this is a taste of the kingdom. Jesus was wooing men to accept the King and kingdom. Most of the parables are found to be con-nected in their first meaning with explaining about the kingdom. The kingdom will follow the law of growth that is common in nature—sowing, waiting, cultivating, and reaping. Its influence will spread gradually until all feel its presence and power. It must meet and deal with the obstacles presented by different men's temperaments and dispositions and temptations. There will be opposition, gradually overcome, but never fully. Many will be carried along by the current of the day. It will be a good current, for righteousness will be the common thing then. But in their hearts many will long for something else, something different.

But to many, the new blessed kingdom message will come as a treasure accidentally stumbled upon, not being looked for, but now valued as very precious. To others it will come as the thing they have been eagerly seeking for, and which satisfies the deepest yearnings. One who has had any touch with the pathetic yearning of years found in non-Christian lands can better appreciate the results of this kind in these glad coming days.

The characteristic spirit of the kingdom stands sharply in contrast with the dominant spirit of our own time. The kingdom is said to belong to those who are *"poor in spirit,"* in whom self-assertion and pride have quite gone out, leaving them humble and lowly in heart. The meek will inherit the earth, and will take down all the walls and fences. The penitent man or woman will be freely received regardless of their past, while the proud will find the doorway too low for their unbending heads.

Rewards in the kingdom will be thought of wholly as evidence of the graciousness of the King. And yet more striking, the rewards given will be the privilege of serving, some more, some less, according as they have become skilled in serving. He who serves most truly will be given preferment. The thing prized above all else will be glad obedience to the King.

It will be seen that the kingdom is to be a time of worldwide evangelization. Indeed this is the purpose of the kingdom. There are two periods of worldwide evangelization in our Lord's planning. The present is the Church time of such evangelizing. This is, of course, one of the main objectives of the Church—to take the message of a crucified risen Christ to all men, so the way may be prepared for His return, and through that for the next period of evangelizing.

The kingdom period of worldwide evangelization is under very different conditions. Then the evil one will be removed from the scene of action, the Holy Spirit will have been poured out upon all flesh, and the moral veil now upon men's eyes will be removed. Redeemed Jews will be a nation of missionaries to all the earth. The redeemed ones in their resurrection bodies will have the blessed privilege of helping. And over all will be the presence and supervision of the King, our Lord Jesus Himself. That will be worldwide evangelization in earnest.

Such is a faint glimpse given in both Old and New Testaments of the kingdom spoken of in these Revelation pages in such few words. Almost the whole Bible lies back of those few words. What a time it will be for this old earth! With renewed fervor our hearts repeat, *"Thy kingdom come."*

One Crown More

William Cowper

Come then, and, added to Thy many crowns,
Receive yet one, the crown of all the earth,
Thou who alone art worthy!
It was Thine by ancient covenant ere nature's birth,
And Thou hast made it Thine by purchase since,
And overpaid its value with Thy blood.
Thy saints proclaim Thee King; and in their hearts
Thy title is engraven with a pen
Dipped in the fountain of eternal love.

The Solitary Saviour

Northcote Deck

"**A**nd *Jesus was left alone*" (Jn. 8:9). The word *"alone"* (*monos*) is used eight times in the Gospels in connection with the Saviour. It truly expresses one aspect of the cost to Him of becoming incarnate in this world of sin. One hesitates to speak of His being lonely; the word hardly seems reverent applied to Him.

MORAL ISOLATION

John 8:9 stresses the moral isolation of the sinless Son of God on His shining way to the cross. That day in Jerusalem, surrounded by a critical crowd of sinners, His searching words so convicted them of sin that they were literally driven, one by one, from His holy presence, till *"Jesus was left alone"* with the woman.

I think that scene gives the clue, and supplies the underlying reason why so often He was alone, isolated by His innate purity and holiness. From eternity He had dwelt *"in the light no man can approach unto"* (1 Tim. 6:16). And in His earthly life this continually compelled that moral solitude, which must have been His experience through the years.

HIS "ADOPTED" FAMILY

He had shrouded His glory, laid aside His riches when He came to earth, but His purity He could not lay aside. But having a body *"prepared"* for Him, His humanity longed for human fellowship. This was largely denied Him. *"God setteth the solitary in families,"* wrote the Psalmist, but the Saviour's natural family failed Him, and His "adopted" spiritual family did not really come into *"the fellowship of His sufferings"* till after He had gone back to heaven, with the result that He was called to tread *"the winepress alone."*

We have only one glimpse of Him as a child, when in Jerusalem His mother discovered Him *"in the midst of the doctors"* (Lk. 2:46). Then the curtain drops, and nothing is revealed of the eighteen hidden years that follow in Nazareth. What did He do and say in those unrecorded years? How did He feel? At least we know how He lived; as ever it was, *"I do always those things that please Him."* We know, too, how He toiled for a living. *"Is not this the carpenter?"* records Mark 6:3. How much that sentence reveals and implies. He did not preach during those silent years of preparation in Nazareth, or they would have remembered it, and not merely referred to Him as *"the carpenter."* No mighty works were done those years either, for the *"beginning of miracles"* was at Cana. *"His hour was not yet come."*

Did He find sympathy in Nazareth with His mission, or fellowship in His solitude? Evidently the common people never realized that in their midst lived One so high and holy, nor shared in His sorrow over sin. His very friends (Mk. 3:21) deemed Him *"beside Himself"* when He began to preach later on. His *"brethren"* too, did not believe in Him (Jn. 7:5) when His ministry began. We must suppose that in earlier years they, too, must have failed Him in real understanding. Even then Psalm 69:8 was being fulfilled: *"I am...a stranger unto...my mother's children."*

MARY, HIS MOTHER

There remains then Mary, His mother. Could He make a real confidant of her? We know at His miraculous birth *"Mary kept all these things and pondered them in her heart"* (Lk. 2:19). And with the doctors Mary *"kept all these sayings in her heart"* (Lk. 2:51). More we are not told. The scene at Cana does imply Mary's perfect confidence in her Son and His power. But does it imply she was His confidant? Had He been able to unburden His heart to her, as to His person and mission, and coming death as sinbearer? Did He find in her that human sympathy which He sought later on? It hardly seems so, even with Mary, for as Psalm 69:20 puts it: *"I looked for some to take pity, but there was none; and for comforters, but I found none."* So for *"about thirty years"* He lived in Nazareth, the solitary Saviour, unrecognized, unknown.

There indeed, day after day, the Lord had been living the Sermon on the Mount years before ever He preached a word of it. Yet, strange to say, that perfect life lived as an example, changed no other lives. It would take the cross to do that.

NAZARETH

Later, when His ministry had begun, He paid a visit to Nazareth, where alone in all the world a perfect human life had been lived; and with what result? We read: *"He could do no mighty work...because of their unbelief"* (Mk. 6:5–6). Pathetic verdict! Thank God He has changed His hometown now, and dwells in the heart of every believer. Yet, alas, though His abode is different, only too often the home conditions are the same; unbelief still is in the heart, hence no mighty work, to His sorrow and our loss. *"Lord, increase our faith."*

Then came His public ministry, and the time when, kindly and deliberately, He had to divest Himself of His earthly relations, for now these natural ties were to be superseded by supernatural ties, and brethren after the flesh had to be replaced by brethren in the Spirit. So, to the seeking mother and brethren (Mt. 12:50) He decreed: *"Whosoever shall do the will of My Father...the same is my brother, and sister, and mother."* So He turned from His natural family to His adopted family. Twelve of them He called to be His disciples. And the function and purpose of these new adopted relations is carefully set forth in Mark 3:14. He ordained twelve that i) they should be with Him, and that ii) He might send them forth to preach. Those words set forth the order of importance of their purpose and call. Their office was to be twofold: they were to share His joys and sorrows with Him; they were to share His salvation with the world.

WITH HIM

Earliest man *"heard the voice of the Lord God walking in the garden in the cool of the day."* Even then, He was seeking fellowship with man. He has been seeking it ever since. The disciples were called *"that they might be with Him."* We too are called (1 Cor. 1:9) *"to the fellowship of His Son Jesus Christ our Lord."* For the highest function and possibility of man must ever be the fellowship of God. Service, however exalted and essential, is after all but a by-product of Christian life. The main, the highest function is fellowship.

Of course we need preparation for it, even as believers. When the prodigal came home, the father did not invite him to sit at the feast in rags. It would not have been fitting, nor was it needful. The loving Father could and did fall on his neck and kiss him, in spite of all his rags. They did not prevent reconciliation. They would prevent communion. Even so there is a fellowship with God which cannot be enjoyed by any believer without suitable apparel, the robe of Christ's righteousness *"put on."* As with the prodigal, this is supplied free, on the terms that we do *"put...on the Lord Jesus Christ"* day by day.

This preparation for fellowship is often long and costly. Many lessons had to be learned by the disciples in their school of prayer. Many must be learned by each of us, yet how well worth the learning! Many indeed are the *"strange ways"* and acts of God. Time, too, is needed, and there is often bewilderment.

Yet there must be patience and trust in the dark. "A saint's life is in the hand of God, like a bow and arrow in the hands of an archer." God is aiming at something the saint cannot see, and He stretches and strains, and every now and then the saint cries: "I cannot stand any more!" God does not heed; He goes on stretching till His purpose is in sight, then He lets fly. You cannot see Him clearly just now, you cannot understand what He is doing, but you know Him. You may often have to trust Him in the dark. So, only, is deepest fellowship developed.

"That they might be with Him." As He said later, they did continue with Him in His temptations; yet only in body; how far off they were in sympathy and understanding! When, *"offended"* at the truth *"many of His disciples...walked no more with Him"* (Jn. 6:66), He cried: *"Will ye also go away?"* Then though Peter made a sincere declaration, *"Thou art the Christ,"* yet when the Saviour spoke of His inevitable cross, Peter, only willing for the crown, cried, *"Be it far from Thee, Lord!"* So, refusing to discuss His death, he failed Him in His need. Later at the transfiguration, sent by God to revive their fainting faith, Moses and Elijah spoke with Him concerning just that, *"His departure,"* and so supplied the disciples' lack.

But why prolong the recital of the disciples' failure and the Saviour's isolation? Only after Pentecost and the gift of the Spirit did the disciples and believers really begin to enter into *"the fellowship of His sufferings."* Was there any sorrow like His sorrow? Can we not make amends today? He has promised to enable us to abide in Him. Thus by the Spirit's aid we may walk in unbroken communion and fellowship with the Saviour. Then, day by day, He may *"see of the travail of His soul and shall be satisfied."*

Alone

Doris Markham

That pathway—O let it be treasured!
For none ever trod it before,
Those steps of aloneness unmeasured
Our spirits must pause and adore.

None, none had been laid in that manger,
And none had been laid in that grave,
But Jesus, the heavenly Stranger,
Who came wayward sinners to save.

Alone in the hall of decision
When judgment was taken away;
Alone on that cross of derision,
Of darkness, distress and dismay.

Alone, apprehended and taken,
While lovers forsook Him and fled;
Alone, and completely forsaken
When judgment was poured on His head.

And yet 'twas for us He endured it;
Alone in perfection was He;
Our blessing, He only secured it,
By dying alone on the tree.

Lord, Thou art no longer deserted!
The Father is sharing His throne
With Thee, who our judgment averted
That we might be never alone.

The First World Conqueror

J. Stanley Collins

World conquest has been the objective of kings, emperors, rulers, and dictators from the dawning of time. Over and over again great empires have arisen to fling their armies ruthlessly on their fellow creatures in order to gain their objective, to claim universal dominion, to place one man on the throne of the world. None have ever succeeded; none ever will.

And yet the world has been conquered. One Man, without an army, without human aid, without human strategy, without the loss of one life, has conquered, and is now waiting to take command.

One morning, as it began to dawn, He stood by the side of an empty tomb. All power in heaven and earth stood vested in Him.

Did I say He accomplished this without the loss of one life? Then I am wrong. One life *was* lost, but it was His. Blood was shed, but it was His. Agony and suffering was endured, but He alone endured it. A battle was fought, but unlike all other would-be world conquerors, He alone knew who to attack, and He alone was strong enough to attack the one who up to His coming was the actual world ruler.

Think of the wars that have been fought, of the millions that have perished. Think of the blood that has been shed. Listen to the sound of martial music, the thunder of thousands of horses, the roll of the drums, the cries of the wounded and the dying, and then remember it was all for nothing. Satan looked on and laughed as men slew their fellowmen by the millions.

From the day that man fell in the Garden of Eden, the authority of Satan as god of this world was never challenged. Weapons stronger than man could forge were needed. No man born of woman could hope to succeed. As every child was born into the world, Satan could lay his hand on its head and say, "mine." But help was forthcoming, and in due time a baby lay in a manger at Bethlehem. The birth of that child caused the greatest joy in heaven, and the greatest consternation in hell. For the first time, Satan found he could not claim a child as his own, for this child had been born sinless.

All the powers of hell were marshalled to destroy Him, but all was useless. The child grew and waxed strong; the overshadowing power of God Almighty was upon Him. Satan saw in that child the One who would one day overthrow his kingdom, wrest from his hand the scepter of authority, and lead out from his power a great multitude that no man could number. From the moment of His birth, every shaft that hell could forge was leveled at Him. All was useless. He stood alone in the wilderness, and there endured every form of temptation that Satan could devise. Satan offered him the world. He would even sacrifice that, if only he could break down the sinless Man who stood before him. Satan knew his time was short. If he could not crush this Man, then this Man would crush him.

Only one sin would suffice to bring Him under Satan's power, and ruin forever the chance of redemption for humanity. The time was drawing near, and although Satan made every attempt possible, Christ could say, as the shadow of the cross fell athwart His path, *"The prince of this world cometh, and hath nothing in Me"* (Jn. 14:30). And so at last the battle joined, and the Christ, having lived a perfect, holy, sinless life, was able and entitled to offer Himself without spot to God to make a way whereby God could be just and justify the ungodly.

Behold Him as He hangs naked, bleeding and alone. He conquered, not with force of arms, not by riding over the bodies of His enemies, not by taking the lives of others, but by giving Himself. Heaven looked down, hushed to silence; more than twelve legions of angels stood ready to come to His aid; all heaven watched while one Man, single-handed, and alone, engaged all the forces of Satan. Then from the darkness of the cross, the cry of the mighty Victor arose: *"It is finished"* (Jn. 19:30).

It echoed through the courts of heaven and blended with the millions of voices raised to extol the Victor. It echoed through the caverns of hell and all there knew that the death-knell of Satan was being sounded.

As the sun rose and illuminated that Figure standing in that garden, it revealed the first world conqueror. From the world He had redeemed, He ascends to heaven. For the first time in the history of the universe, a Man is seen entering heaven, clothed with a vesture dipped in blood. His hands, feet, side and brow bear the honored wounds of the battle. No one dare stop His entry—the everlasting doors swing open, and slowly He proceeds through the gathering and exulting millions. He approaches the very throne of God by whose side there is the empty seat He vacated thirty or more years before. He ascends the throne and takes His place at the right hand of God, and He is there now—waiting until His enemies be made His footstool, for *"He must reign until He hath put all enemies under His feet."* When that happens, when the last enemy, Death, is conquered, He shall be invited to take His own throne when *"The kingdoms of this world are become the kingdoms of our Lord, and of His Christ; and He shall reign for ever and ever"* (Rev. 11:15).

Our Conquering King

Isaac Watts

Hosanna to our conquering King!
The prince of darkness flies;
His troops rush headlong down to hell,
Like lightning from the skies.

There, bound in chains, the lions roar,
And fright the rescued sheep;
But heavy bars confine their power
And malice to the deep.

Hosanna to our conquering King!
All hail, incarnate Love!
Ten thousand songs and glories wait
To crown Thy head above.

Thy victories and Thy deathless fame
Through the wide world shall run,
And everlasting ages sing
The triumphs Thou hast won.

The Fragrance of Christ

E. F. Harrison

 "*He is altogether lovely...Thy name is as ointment poured forth*" (Song of Sol. 5:16; 1:3).

Bread and water are necessities of life. It is no wonder, then, that the Scripture sets forth Christ as the Bread of Life and assures that if any man thirst, he may come unto Him and drink. But bread and water may indicate a very limited existence. We have come to associate such a diet with a life whose horizon is limited by iron bars. Christ is our necessary spiritual food, but He is more. The Chinese proverb says, "If you have two loaves of bread, sell one and buy a lily." Our Beloved One has a loveliness which entrances us, a fragrance which draws out our purest delight.

Perfume is considered a luxury item. The disciples, witnesses to what they considered extravagant excess, exclaimed, *"Why was this waste made?"* The money from the perfume lavished on the Lord could have been given to charity, they suggested. No, responded the Saviour. This was not waste; this was worship.

Perfumes are either free or extracted. In the rose, for example, the odoriferous oils exist in volatile form, passing continually into the atmosphere. In resins, on the other hand, the fragrance is set free only after a process of extraction. Our Rose of Sharon, unexcelled for beauty and fragrance, is available to all, for He is the Gift of God to the entire world. He did not need to be pressed or forced; the sweetness of His life passed continually into the lives of those around Him.

He is altogether lovely. There is no blight upon this rose. There is no fly in this ointment. Nowhere else is such perfection to be found. Even as the world about us has its wilderness places, so every human life has its dark and barren spots, tokens of failure. Every human idol eventually totters and falls. The dearest and best we know among our fellows cannot satisfy our craving for the highest fellowship. But no Christian has ever been able to say truthfully that he has grown tired of the fellowship of his Lord, or that He has failed to satisfy the believing heart.

The Lord Jesus is lovely in the estimation of the Father. *"This is My beloved Son, in whom I am well pleased."* The Son offered Himself without spot or blemish as the whole burnt offering, committed in heart and purpose to doing the will of God, even though it meant Calvary. He is the sweet savor that satisfies God's heart.

He is lovely, too, in the eyes of those who know Him as their Saviour and Friend. Our hearts gladly concur in the conclusion of one who saw much of Him and leaned upon His breast: *"full of grace and truth."* He had loveliness of speech. Needing at times to speak words of earnest denunciation, yet He spoke them without curling His lips in scorn. His gentleness invited little children to His arms' embrace. His words of peace when His followers were anxious and distraught imparted a benediction which lingers upon His Church even now.

He had loveliness of compassion. The condition of the unshepherded multitudes stirred His soul with strong emotion. Though He knew they would turn from Him in His hour of deep anguish, He would never think of turning from them. If the Pharisees would come to embarrass Him, He would stoop and avert His eyes so as not to embarrass them. Would they come to scorn and argue, to reject Him, He would tell them of the other brother who was as welcome in the Father's house as the prodigal.

On that occasion when the house was *"filled"* with the fragrance of the perfume, there were nonetheless two places where the aroma was strongest: the Saviour's feet and the woman's hair. May our lives be in such intimate contact with Him that the same fragrance will linger in our lives, and that it may be said of us as it was said of the early believers: *"...they took knowledge of them, that they had been with Jesus"* (Acts 4:13).

Love's Lingering Sweetness

E. J. McBride (1867-1949)

"Passing through the valley of Baca, [they] make it a well-spring"
Psalm 84:6

If Baca's valley proves a well to me
It is because my Father's will I see;
Proving that love behind each sorrow dwells,
And sorrow's pathway only mercy spells.
Love's pressure brings out fragrance rare and sweet
Because, beneath the weight, Himself I meet;
And in the sunshine of His blessed face
There flows from me some answer to His grace.
Then chastening proves the love remains the same
As when it first to plow its furrows came;
But room is left, when self is turned aside,
To let the fragrance of that love abide.

Christ the Redeemer

Author Unknown

No place touches us with a more melancholy sense of the fleeting nature of earthly glory than an old deserted castle. All is gone but the main keep. Stoutly battling with time, as one not easily subdued, it stands erect in its ruin amid the grass-green mounds, that, like graves of the past, show where other buildings once have stood. Gray with moss, or mantled with ivy, the strong thick walls are slowly mouldering; and there is deep desolation in these silent courts. No step but our own treads the floor that in other days shook to the dancers' feet; nor sound is heard in halls which once rung with music, and sweet voices, and merry laughter, but the moaning wind, which seems to wail for the wreck around it; or the sudden rush and flapping of some startled bird that flies at our intrusion from her lonely nest.

If happily an empty chain hangs rusting in the dungeon where captives once had pined, how cold the hearth around whose roaring fires in long winter nights many a tale was told, and many a bright group had gathered, and the mother nursed her babe, and the father told his rapt and listening boys of stirring scenes in flood and field!

In the grass-grown court below, where once they had mustered gloriously for the bridal day, or grim for battle, the sheep are quietly feeding. And here on the battlement some pine, or birch, or mountain ash, rooted in a crevice and fed by decay, lifts its stunted form, where the banner of an ancient house floated proudly in days of old, or spread itself out, defiant, as the fight raged around the beleaguered walls, and the war-cry of assailants without was answered by the cheers of gallant men within.

Now all is changed—the stage a ruin, spectators and actors gone. They sleep in the grave; their loves, and wars, their fears, and joys, and sorrows—where ours, too, soon shall be—buried in oblivion.

> *Their memory and their name is gone,*
> *Alike unknowing and unknown.*

And, greatest change of all, the heirs of those who reared that massy pile, and rode helmed to battle with a thousand vassals at their back, have sunk amid the wrecks of fortune. Fallen into meanness and obscurity, as humble rustics, they now, perhaps, plow the lands which once their fathers held.

Such changes have happened in our country. But changes corresponding to these never happened in ancient Israel. It was there, as in the heavens above us, whose luminaries, after a certain period of time has elapsed, always return to the same place in the firmament, and the same relative position to each other. The sun, for instance—although changing its place daily—shall rise and set, twelve months from this date, at the same hour, and appear at his meridian in the same spot as today.

Corresponding to that, society—whatever change meanwhile took place in personal liberty or hereditary property—returned among the old Hebrews to the very same state in which it was at the commencement of those fifty years, whose close brought in the jubilee.

> *"Then,"* said Moses, *"shalt thou cause the trumpet of the jubilee to sound on the tenth day of the seventh month, in the day of atonement shall ye make the trumpet sound throughout all your land. And ye shall hallow the fiftieth year, and proclaim liberty throughout all the land unto all the inhabitants thereof; it shall be a jubilee unto you; and ye shall return every man unto his possession, and ye shall return every man unto his family"* (Lev. 25:9–10).

In consequence either of his crimes or his misfortunes, the Hebrew was occasionally obliged to part with his paternal estate. His was sometimes a still greater calamity; for not only was his property sold, but his liberty. He became the bond-servant of some more fortunate brother. So matters stood till the fiftieth year arrived, and the jubilee was blown. At that trumpet sound—how fondly anticipated! how gladly heard!—the fetters fall from his limbs, and the slave of yesterday is today a freeman. At that trumpet sound the beggar doffs his rags, the weary laborer throws down his tools. Marriage bells never rang so merry as that blessed peal; it has changed the serf into a freeholder, a man of substance and position.

And as, blown with the breath of liberty, trumpet replied to trumpet, and the sound of the jubilee, rising from valley to mountain, echoed among the rocky hills, and spread itself over the land from beyond Jordan's bank to the shores of the sea, from the roots of snowy Lebanon to the burning desert—every man bade adieu to beggary and wandering and exile. Like parted streams, divided families were reunited; long alienated possessions were restored to their original owners; and, amid universal rejoicings, feastings and music, every man returned to spend the rest of his days in his father's house, and when he died, to mingle his own with ancestral dust.

What a singular institution! As a civil arrangement, acting as a check both on excessive wealth and on excessive poverty, it was without a parallel in any ancient or modern nation. But it was more; it was a symbolic institution. More than in many respects a great social blessing, it had a deep, holy, spiritual meaning. Celebrated on the great day of atonement—that day when the goat, typical of our Lord Jesus, bore away the sins of the people—it was the symbol of a better restitution and a better redemption. It was, in fact, a striking, very beautiful figure of the redemption which we have through the blood of Christ—even the forgiveness of sins.

Before turning your attention to the redemption, of which that jubilee was such a remarkable figure, let me by way of warning remark: Our redemption is not, like that of the Hebrews, a simple matter of time.

Every fifty years, and in certain cases every seven years, redeemed the Hebrew, and restored him to the enjoyment of his property.

> *"If thy brother,"* said God, *"an Hebrew man, or an Hebrew woman, be sold unto thee, and serve thee six years; then in the seventh year thou shalt let him go free from thee. And when thou sendest him out free from thee, thou shalt not let him go away empty"* (Lev. 15:12–13).

Thus, time set free the Hebrew slave, and, as its finger moved over the face of the sun-dial, pointed him onwards to freedom. Everywhere, and in its most ordinary course, time works many changes—the young grow old, and raven locks grow gray; the poor rise into wealth, while the rich sink into poverty. Old families disappear, and new ones start up. And, constantly changing the condition of society, as he turns the wheel of fortune, Time is altering the form even of this great globe itself. The proudest mountains are bending before his scepter, and yielding to his silent but resistless sway.

Nor is there a tiny stream that trickles over the rock, and, often hid under the broad fern and nodding grasses and wild flowers that grow on its narrow banks, betrays itself only by the gentle murmur with which it descends to join the river that receives its tribute, and rolls it onward to the ocean, but—teaching us in the highest matters not to despise the day of small things—is wearing down the mountain, and filling up the sea. Through the agencies of heat and cold, dews and rains, summer showers and winter snows, time is remodelling the features of our world, and—perhaps in that symbolizing the onward progress and future condition of society—reducing its various inequalities to one great common level.

But amid these changes shall years change, as a matter of course, the condition of a sinner? Shall they redeem him, for instance, from his slavery, or even relax the chains of sin? In the course of time you will grow older, but not of necessity better. On the contrary, while the Hebrew slave was, by every year and day he lived, brought nearer to redemption, and could say, on such a day and at such an hour I shall be free, it is a solemn and awful fact, that the longer you live in sin, the more distant, more difficult, more hopeless, does your salvation become. *"The last state of that man is worse than the first."*

Let us not flatter ourselves with the very common hope: I shall grow better as I grow older. That is very unlikely to happen. The unconverted are less likely to be saved at the jubilee age of fifty than at twenty-five; in their seventieth than in their seventh year. *"Oh that they were wise, that they understood this, that they would consider their latter end!"* (Deut. 32:29).

Do you say, in reply, But what then am I to do? Can I redeem myself? Assuredly not. But are we, because we can be redeemed only through the blood of Christ, to sit still; as if that redemption would come like a jubilee in the common course of providence, or time, or nature? No. We are to be up and doing; since, in a sense, it is as true of a soul's as of a nation's liberty: "Who would be free, themselves must strike the blow."

I do not say that we are to rise like an oppressed nation which wrings its liberties from a tyrant's hand; nor that we can purchase redemption, as we bought with our millions the freedom of West Indian slaves; nor that through works of righteousness that we do or have done, we can establish any claim whatever to its blessings. By care and industry you may acquire goods, not goodness; money, but never merit—merit in the sight of God. And yet I say, in God's name:

Labor not for the meat which perisheth but for that meat which endureth unto everlasting life (Jn. 6:27);
Work out your own salvation with fear and trembling (Phil. 2:12);
Give diligence to make your calling and election sure (2 Pet. 1:10);
Take diligent heed to do the commandment and the law, to love the Lord your God, and to walk in all His ways, and to keep His commandments, and to cleave unto Him, and to serve Him with all your heart, and with all your soul (Josh. 22:5).

There are various ways of being diligent. One man, seated at the loom, is busy with the shuttle; another, at the desk, with his pen; another, in the field, at his plow; another bends to the oar, and, plowing the deep, reaps his harvest on the stormy waters; another, seen through the smoke of battle, is straining all his energies on the bloody field, winning honors with the bayonet's rush and at the cannon's mouth. And, though men may call him idle, yonder poor beggar, who, an orphan child or infirm old man, claims our pity and reproves our indolence, is also diligent as the others. His hand is not idle, it is busy knocking; nor are his feet, they bear him weary from house to house, from door to door; nor is his tongue, it pleads his poverty, and tells his tale of sorrow. While pressed by necessity and earnest of purpose, out of his hollow eyes he throws such looks of misery as move compassion and melt the heart.

And such as that suppliant's, along with the use of other means, are the labors, the diligence, to which God's gracious mercy and your own necessities call you. Unable to save yourselves, be it yours to besiege with prayers the throne of grace. Learn from Simon Peter what to do, and where to turn; not Peter sleeping in the garden, but

Peter sinking in the sea. One who in his boyhood had learned to breast the billow, and feel at home upon the deep, he makes no attempt to swim. The shore lies beyond his reach, nor can the boldest swimmer live amid these swelling waters. His companions cannot save him; their boat, unmanageable, drifts before the gale, and they cannot save themselves. He turns his back on them. He directs no look, nor cry to them; but, fixing his eyes on that divine form which, calm, unmoved, master of the tempest, steps majestically from billow to billow, the drowning man throws out his arms to Jesus, and cries: *"Lord, save me."* Did he cry in vain? No more shall you. Jesus came to seek and to save that which was lost; nor did He ever say unto any of the sons of men, *"Seek ye Me in vain."*

He offered His soul for sin, and came to redeem us from all iniquity. Consider Christ as the Redeemer; not as *a* Redeemer, but *the* Redeemer. There is no other. *"There is none other name under heaven given among men, whereby we must be saved."* All the types and symbols of the Saviour teach you this. There was one ark in the flood—but one; and all perished except those who sailed in it. There was one altar in the temple—but one; and no sacrifices were accepted but those offered there— *"the altar,"* as the Bible says, that *"sanctified the gift."* There was one way through the depths of the Red Sea—but one; and only where the water, held back by the hand of God, stood up in crystal walls, was a passage opened for those that were ready to perish. And even so, there is but *"one mediator between God and men, the man Christ Jesus."*

Since He is the only Saviour, and the work to save your soul was accomplished when He cried, *"It is finished,"* what then is this work that you must do? Some in Christ's day on earth asked the same question: *"What shall we do, that we might work the works of God? Jesus answered and said unto them, This is the work of God, that ye believe on Him whom He hath sent"* (Jn. 6:28-29). The work the sinner is called upon to do is not meritorious; all merit resides in the precious blood of Christ. But it is essential to enter into the good of the redemption He has provided, *"...the righteousness of God which is by faith of Jesus Christ unto all and upon all them that believe"* (Rom. 3:22).

Change of Raiment

Gerhard Ter Steegen (1697-1769)

Lord Jesus, all my sin and guilt
Love laid of old on Thee,
Thy love the cross and sorrow willed,
Love undeserved by me.

For as I am to Thee I come,
I clasp Thy blessed feet,
And learn the mystery of love
So deep, so sweet.

Enfolded, O my Lord, in Thee,
And hid in Thee I rest,
Enwrapped in Christ's own purity,
Secure upon Thy breast.

Had I an angel's raiment fair
With heavenly gems unpriced,
That glorious garb I would not wear—
My robe is Christ.

The Hidden Years

G. Campbell Morgan

We must clearly understand that man can only enter the life of Jesus by the way of His death; that death being the gate, not only to eternal life, as it stretches beyond this place and time of conflict, but also to the eternal life which we live today, in direct and positive communion with Him.

Having known Him as the Saviour and having at the cross found our way into the realm of life, He then becomes our example, and all that He is in the revelation of the fourfold Gospel marks His intention for His people, for He wills that they should be like Him.

It is not given to every man or woman to serve God in public places; the great majority live their lives outside any prominent sphere, and as part of a very small circle of relatives and acquaintances. I want to know what there is in the life of Jesus helpful to the individuals that compose these crowds.

We are accustomed to think of Him as one in public ministry, as the man of the marketplace and the crowd, but the greater part of His life was not lived in those places where we have grown most familiar with Him, but in that quiet seclusion where most men and women will always live. Yet how little we know concerning that period, how meager is the biblical information. I do not say it is not enough. I believe it is enough, but in the mere matter of words, how small it is. I have the story of His birth, and then I lose sight of Him for twelve years. Then I see Him again going out to His Jewish confirmation, asking questions of the doctors and hearing them. A wonderful glimpse, a glittering flash, and then I lose Him again for eighteen years, at the end of which time He comes to be baptized by John in Jordan, and begins His public ministry.

What of those years? Where was He? What was He doing? Let us try and see Him in those hidden years. Take these two statements: *"Thou art My beloved Son; in Thee I am well pleased"*; and *"Is not this the carpenter?"* They supply the story of the eighteen years.

JESUS WAS A CARPENTER PLEASING GOD. But is it fair to put them together like that? I think you will see that it is. Upon what occasion did that divine voice speak? On the occasion of the baptism. Jesus had left behind all the doings of those quiet, peaceful years, and was at the dividing line between private and public life. And there, at the parting of the ways, God lit up all the years that had gone with the sweet words of approval, *"Thou art My beloved Son; in Thee **I am well pleased**."* Whatever else I know, or do not know, about the hidden years of the life of Jesus, this one thing is certain, that through them all He pleased God. After that pronouncement, He went to the wilderness and was tempted, and after that He went to Nazareth, the place where He had been brought up. It was a small town, a kind of hamlet on the hillside, of perhaps three thousand inhabitants.

This young man comes back to His boyhood's home, where everyone knows Him. He goes to the synagogue as was His custom on the Sabbath day, and reads out of the book. Then He talks to the assembled people, and they look at Him, and listen, wonder depicted on their faces. Can you not see the picture? That little synagogue, the old Jewish people with keen faces watching the speaker, and then turning to each other, saying, *"Whence hath this man these things? We know Him perfectly well; He is the carpenter."* Yes, they know Him; they have watched Him toiling day after day, month after month, in the workshop, bending over the bench with the tools of His craft in His hand. They cannot account for Him as a teacher because they did not account for Him as a toiler.

Mark then tells what these people said about Him. Other men made the blunder of saying He was the son of the carpenter, but these men light up for us the eighteen years by asking, *"Is not this the carpenter?"* I have now two facts concerning this period. I have the testimony of the men who knew Him best, and the testimony of God who knew Him better even than they.

Let us first take the human declaration, *"Is not this the carpenter?"* and hold it in the light of the divine, *"In Thee I am well pleased"*; then let us take the divine, *"Thou art My beloved Son,"* and hold it in the light of the human, *"Is not this the carpenter?"*

For the greater part of the life of Jesus, He worked with His own hands for His own living. That brings the Son of God, in living, pulsating life, close to every man who works. Oh! that we may derive the strength and comfort from this fact which it is calculated to afford. Businessmen, you who have been at work all the week and have been harassed by daily labors. Are you weary and seeking for new inspiration? This Jesus was not a king upon a throne; He was not for the greater part of His life a teacher, with the thrill and excitement of public life to buoy Him up. No, the long years ran on, and He was doing what some of you speak of as "the daily round, the common task." The man Jesus rose at daybreak, and, picking up His tools, made yokes and tables in order that He might have something to eat, and that, not for a brief period, but for eighteen years. He was an apprentice boy, a young man using His craft, a master in His little shop, with the shavings round Him and the tools about Him.

That is the human picture. But that human picture becomes supremely precious to me as the light of the divine falls upon it. The eighteen years are over, the tools are laid aside, His feet will no more make music as He walks among the rustling shavings. God says, *"I am...pleased."* It meant that Jesus had never done in that carpenter's shop a piece of shoddy work. When Jesus sent out yokes that the farmers would use, they were so fashioned that they would gall no ox. *"Take My yoke upon you"* gathers force as an illustration from the fidelity of the carpenter's shop.

Sometimes we have overshadowed the carpenter's shop with Calvary's cross. We have no right to do it. We have come to forget the fidelity of the Son of God in the little details of life, as we have gazed upon His magnificent triumphs in the places of passion and conflict. We should ever remember that the final triumph was the natural outcome of the victories won in little things.

Who is this coming up out of the waters of baptism, upon whom the dove hovers and settles, and concerning whom Heaven's voice is heard to speak? God marks Him out here from all His fellowmen: *"Thou art My beloved Son."* He is the anointed of God. He is the one personage who is charged with the great mission of restoring the kingdom of God. God marks Him in that great word as His appointed Messiah, as Shiloh, as the Daysman from on high, as the Day-spring. And now He is standing on the banks of Jordan, and we look upon Him for the first time with amazement and astonishment, and wonder if this be the beloved Son of God, what has He been doing, where has He been in the years preceding this public manifestation?

Come back again to the question, *"Is not this the carpenter?"* and the wonder is presented from a new standpoint. The Son of God, charged with the greatest commission that any being in heaven or earth has ever had to bear, was for eighteen years at work in a carpenter's shop. We hardly see the wonder of this until we look more closely at it. I may be speaking to some young man upon whose heart is lying the burden of India, the need of China, of Africa. You are touched with the sacrificial passion of the Son of God to go, and yet God has shut you up here at home. You have to live and care for a sick one; you cannot go. The desire is there, but the door is not open. It is only those who know something of what that experience is who can understand the strange marvel of the Son of God, commissioned to do the work that precedes your passion, the infinitely greater work, and yet with that passion upon Him, every morning He goes to the carpenter's shop, every night goes home to rest. What does it mean? How is it that He, the beloved of God, the anointed of God, can be—there is no irreverence in saying it—content?

The answer is here. Jesus lived in the power of the truth which we are so slow to learn, that there is something infinitely better than doing a great thing for God—to be where God wants us to be, to do what God wants us to do, and to have no will apart from His. Jesus understood that. The carpenter's shop was the will of God for Him. Now do not misunderstand me. From the illustration I used a moment ago, you may come to think that I intend to say Jesus did it as a duty while He longed for the cross. Nothing of the kind. *"I delight to do Thy will, O My God."*

I am going to ask you to press this question a little further. Was this a capricious matter, this will of God for Jesus? Does it not look hard and arbitrary that God should have put Him to such common labor? Why not let Him face the conflict and get the victory, and return to heaven? There was a deep necessity in the whole arrangement. In that carpenter's shop He fought my battles. My hardest fight is never fought when there is a crowd to applaud, but when I am alone. Now that was what Jesus was doing for eighteen years. There was no crowd to sing "Hosanna." Alone He did His work and faced all the subtle forms of temptation that beset humankind, and one by one He put His conquering foot upon the neck of them, until the last was baffled and beaten, and His enemies were palsied by the strong stroke of His pure right arm. That is what He was doing.

I never come to this story of the early years and read what these men of Nazareth said about Him without learning how dangerous it is to pronounce my little sentence upon any single human life.

Oh! men of Nazareth, down in that carpenter's shop that you pass and repass, where you sometimes pause and look in and see Him at His work, there is the One who spoke and it was done, who put His compass upon the deep, who fashioned all things by the word of His power. You have never seen Him, never known Him, and your estimate of Him is that He is one of you—only a carpenter. Job's judges and Christ's critics are on a level, and they are on a level with everyone of us who tries to pass his sentences upon his fellow men.

But I gather not only this relative lesson; there are personal lessons. The first is this: the phrase "common task" should be struck out of every life. Jesus taught us that all toil is holy, if the toiler be holy. Not for the sake of controversy, but as a protest against a misconception of human life, I tell you that no man has any right, simply because he preaches or performs certain functions, to speak of himself as a man in "holy orders." The man who goes out to work tomorrow morning with his bag on his back, and his tools in it, if he be a holy man, has claims to that distinction, and if that man goes down into the carpenter's shop and saws a piece of timber, the saw is a vessel of the sanctuary of God if the man is a priest who uses it.

All service is sacred service. Carry this thought of the working Christ into all the days of the coming week, behind the counter and in the office, and, beloved sisters, in the home also. If every businessman wrote his letters as though Jesus would have to look over them, what lovely letters we should have. I do not know that they would have tracts in them; that is not my point, but they would be true, robust, honest letters. Oh! you men, won't you do your business for Christ? Sisters, won't you take the home and make it a holy place for the shining of the Shekinah? If Christ lived the larger part of His life working, then our work is lit with a new beauty.

I learn this lesson also, that no man is fit for the great places of service who has not fitted himself by fidelity in obscurity. You want, you tell me, to preach the gospel in China. Are you living it at home? God does not want men or women to preach His gospel anywhere who have not made it shine in their own homes. I do not ask, "Can you do the great work that hangs upon your hearts?" but "Are you doing the present work faithfully?" What we want is to feel that if we are to do a big thing in the public service, we must be true in the small things of life. The Carpenter's shop made Calvary not a battlefield merely, but a day of triumph that lit heaven and earth with hope, and if you and I would triumph when our crisis comes, we must triumph in the little things of the common hours.

Thirty Silent Years

Ora Rowan (1834-1879)

O restless, hasty heart,
Oft checked in bitter tears,
What lesson hast thou here to learn
From all those thirty years?

Behold the perfect Man,
God's purpose full in view,
Thus waiting hidden and unknown,
With such a work to do!

He knowing well the plan
Hastes not to tread the road,
But waits in patience for the sign,
Dependent upon God.

Lesson of priceless worth,
Those thirty silent years!
Rebuke to nature's anxious zeal,
Its haste, its restless fears!

The peaceful, quiet mind
That needs no checking rod,
The patient dignity of faith
That dares to wait on God!

No rash, unchastened zeal,
Pressing to do His will;
The heart that knows His guiding
Awaits it, and is still.

O wondrous thirty years!
Thus teach my restless heart,
If 'tis so blest to work for Him,
Blest too the waiting part!

How sweet the quiet trust,
Those secret times with God!
Though friends around misunderstand,
Though Satan stalks abroad.

The heart in untouched calm
With Him waits patiently;
O lesson of those thirty years,
I thank my God for thee!

The Victor and the Vanquished

J. R. MacDuff

I f ever there was a case which we might have thought would have repelled Infinite Goodness and Infinite Purity, it is that described by the story of the demoniac in Luke 8. No leper-house more loathsome or polluted than this! Joined to his filthy idols—the trail of the serpent in every chamber of imagery—Christ might well have said, *"Let him alone!"*

But who can limit the Holy One of Israel? He would leave behind in that wild region—even if He never visited it again—one enduring memorial of His grace and power. He would tell people in every age that if Satan is mighty, there is a mightier still; that over this Legion dominion *"all power"* is committed to the *"Stronger than the strong man."* He has only to utter the word, and the demons surrender their prey, crouching submissive at His feet!

Moreover, declaring a still further exhibition of the Saviour's power in the sequel of the narrative, observe the demons would not and dared not enter into the herd of swine until they had received His permissive word, *"Go."* Blessed assurance! Satan's power is bounded! Satan's Lord says as then, *"Hitherto shalt thou come, but no further, and here shall thy proud waves be stayed!"* (Job 38:11).

Both from the case of this Gadarene demoniac and the one in the synagogue of Capernaum, we learn that, great as was the sway of Satan over the bodies and souls of men, it was not such as to prevent them taking themselves to Jesus, and seeking His mercy. We may take comfort in the assurance that no power of Satan can deter us fleeing to the One who is the *"Power of God."* If our faith and hope is built on that Rock, *"the gates of hell shall not prevail against it."*

Further, we have the assurance that there is a period of triumph at hand—a time coming when Satan's kingdom shall be destroyed, when Jesus shall put him and all other enemies *"under His feet."*

That Satanic Empire got its greatest and final blow on the cross of Calvary. *"Now,"* said Jesus, when that cross was projecting its shadow on His path, "Now shall the Prince of this world be cast out!" And it was so. As He bowed His head and cried, *"It is finished,"* he dragged the pillars of the Usurper's Empire to the dust. And if *"we see not yet all things put under Him,"* we know on infallible authority that victory does await the Prince of life. The chain is already forged which is to bind the destroyer. Ever since the day when his serried legions were routed at Calvary, the loyal subjects of his Divine Conqueror have been following up the triumph of their Lord, gathering spoils and trophies from the nations so long enthralled. The Great Captain of Salvation *"from henceforth [is] expecting, until His enemies be made His footstool."*

You who are feeling at times downcast by reason of *"the depths of Satan,"* mourning over his power alike in your own hearts, in the church of God, and in the world; remember his doom is sealed! Jesus can say of each one of His people as of Gad of old, *"A troop shall overcome him, but he shall overcome at the last."* We can anticipate with confidence the predicted period when the tyranny of six thousand years shall end—Satan and all his discomfited legions be strewn, like the hosts of Egypt, on the shores of Time—and, in the words of God to His people, *"The [enemies] ye have seen today, ye shall see no more forever"* (Ex. 14:13).

Stronger than the Strong Man

George Lansing Taylor

Naked, scarred with stones, and chains,
Rent by superhuman might,
Frantic with infernal pains,
Here he wanders day and night.

None can tame him, none assuage
Such immeasurable woe;
Love forsakes such fiendish rage,
No man dares that way to go.

Lost to mortal sympathy,
Sundered from the human race,
Evermore his moan and cry
In this sad and dreary place.

But when Christ from far they know,
Filled with trembling fear they fly;
Dreading instant, endless woe,
Prostrate at His feet they cry:

"What have we to do with Thee,
Jesus, Son of God most high?
Must we back to darkness flee?
Chained in fiery tortures lie?"

"What's thy name?" the Saviour asked,
While the listeners shook with fear.
"Legion!" cried the demons masked,
"For a host of us is here."

Sitting clothed at Jesus' feet,
Lo! the maniac now they find;
Glad his former friends to greet,
Sound in body, soul, and mind.

"Leave, oh leave our coasts," they say,
"Let us as aforetime dwell;
Thou hast brought us loss this day;
Ruined what we rear and sell!"

Fit for demons such a land!
Jesus leaves it, filled with woe;
As He leaves at their demand,
The restored one pleads to go.

"No; stay home and tell your kin
All God's goodness shown in this";
Straight with joy he does begin,
Startling all Decapolis.

And oh! all-conquering proof, may we
Know power like this by grace divine;
That Christ may lead in victory,
And in our lives His triumph shine.

Thinking of Christ

John C. Ryle

We ought to think of Christ because of *the office He fills* between God and man. He is the eternal Son of God, through whom alone the Father can be known, approached, and served. He is the Mediator between God and man, through whom alone we can be reconciled to God, pardoned, justified, and saved. He is the divine Person whom God the Father has sealed to be the giver of everything that man requires for his soul. In His favor is life. There is no person of such immense importance to all men.

All men ought to think of Christ because of *what He has done.* He kindly set His thoughts on humanity when man was lost, bankrupt, and helpless, and undertook to save sinners. In the fullness of time, He was born of Mary, and lived thirty-three years in this evil world. At the end of that, He shed His life-blood to pay man's debt to God. He was made a curse, that man might be blessed. He died, that man might live. He was counted a sinner, that man might be counted righteous. If Christ had not died, we would await the wrath of God.

Time is too short to set down all the reasons why men ought to think of Christ. Christ is the grand subject of the Bible; Christ is the great object to whom all Christians give honor; Christ is the end and substance of the ordinances; Christ is the great source of light, peace and hope. There is not a spark of spiritual comfort that has ever illumined a sinner's heart that has not come from Christ. There is no one in whom the world has such a deep interest. There is no one to whom all the world owes so much—high and low, rich and poor, old and young, gentle and simple—all ought to think about Christ.

COMMON THOUGHTS OF MANY ABOUT CHRIST

There were many strange thoughts about Christ when He was on

159

earth. There are still many strange and wrong thoughts about Christ now that He is in heaven.

The thoughts of some people about Christ are simply blasphemous. They are not ashamed to deny His divinity. They refuse to believe the miracles recorded of Him. They tell us that He ought to be ranked with great reformers and philosophers, like Socrates, Seneca, and Confucius, but no higher. There is not the slightest comparison to be made between Christ and any other teacher that ever lived. The difference between Him and others is a gulf that cannot be spanned. It is akin to the difference between gold and clay, between the sun and a candle. Nothing can account for Christ and Christianity but the belief that Christ is God.

The thoughts of some men about Christ are mean and low. They consider that if they do their best, and live moral lives, and go to church pretty regularly, Christ will deal mercifully with them at last, and make up any deficiencies. Thoughts such as these utterly fail to explain why Christ died on the cross. They take the crown off Christ's head. They overthrow the whole system of the gospel, and pull up all its leading doctrines by the roots. They exalt man to an absurdly high position; as if he could pay some part of the price of his soul. They rob man of all the comforts of the gospel, and place the cross in a degraded and inferior position.

THOUGHTS OF TRUE CHRISTIANS ABOUT CHRIST

True Christians have *high thoughts* about Christ. They see in Him a wondrous Person, far above all other beings in His nature—a Person who is at one and the same time perfect God, mighty to save, and perfect man, able to feel. They see in Him an all-powerful Redeemer, who has paid their countless debts to God, and delivered their souls from guilt and hell.

They see in Him an almighty Friend, who left heaven for them, died for them, rose again for them that He might save them forevermore. They see in Him an almighty Physician, who took away their sins in His own blood, put His own Spirit in their hearts, delivered them from the power of sin, and gave them the right to become God's children. Happy are they who have such thoughts!

True Christians have *trustful thoughts* of Christ. They daily lean the weight of their souls on Him by faith for pardon and peace. They daily cling to Him by faith, as a child in a crowd clings to its mother's hand. They daily look to Him for grace, comfort, and strength.

Christ is the Rock under their feet and the staff in their hand, their ark and their city of refuge, their sun and their shield, their health and their light, their life, their hope, and their all. Happy are they who have such thoughts!

True Christians have *experimental thoughts* of Christ. The things that they think of Him they do not merely think with their heads. They have not learned them from schools or picked them up from others. They think them because they have found them true by their own hearts' experience. They have proved them, tasted them, tried them.

They think out what they have felt for themselves. There is all the difference in the world between knowing that a man is a doctor while we never have occasion to employ him, and knowing him as "our own" because we have gone to him for medicine. Similarly, there is a wide difference between head knowledge and experimental thoughts about Christ. Happy are they who have such thoughts.

Christians have *hopeful thoughts* about Christ. They expect to receive from Him far more than they have ever yet received. They look forward to Christ's Second Coming, and expect that then they will see far more than they have seen, and enjoy far more than they have yet enjoyed. They have the earnest of an inheritance now, but they hope for a fuller possession when this world has passed away.

Some of them know more of Him and some of them know less. But all true Christians have learned something about Him. They do not always find such thoughts equally fresh and green in their minds. They have their winter as well as their summer, and their low tide as well as their high water. In other things they may be unable to agree and see alike. But they all agree in their thoughts about Christ. One word they can all say, which is the same in every tongue: that word is *Hallelujah!* Praise to the Lord Christ! One answer they can all make, which in every tongue is equally the same: that word is *"Amen,"* so be it.

Tried, Precious and Sure

Frances Ridley Havergal

Through the yesterday of ages,
Jesus, Thou hast been the same;
Through our own life's checkered pages
Still the one dear changeless name.
Well may we in Thee confide,
Faithful Saviour, proved and tried!

Joyfully we stand and witness
Thou art still today the same;
In Thy perfect, glorious fitness
Meeting every need and claim.
Chiefest of ten thousand Thou!
Saviour, O most precious now.

Gazing down the far forever,
Brighter glows the one sweet Name,
Steadfast radiance, paling never,
Jesus, Jesus! still the same.
Evermore Thou shalt endure,
Our own Saviour, strong and sure!

Wonderful

Arno C. Gabelein

"*And His name shall be called Wonderful...*" (Isa. 9:6).

No mind can fathom, no heart can grasp, no pen describe how wonderful the Saviour is. He is wonderful if we think of Him as the only Begotten of the Father. He is the image of the invisible God, the brightness of His glory and the express image of His Person. How wonderful such a One, who ever was, with no beginning, one with God!

How wonderful His condescension that He who created the angels should be made lower than the angels and lay His glory by, to appear in the form of man on earth!

Wonderful is He in His incarnation, *"that holy Thing,"* as the angel announced Him, truly God and Man. Born of the woman, resting on the bosom of the virgin as a little child, and yet He is the One who ever is in the bosom of the Father.

Wonderful was that blessed life He lived on earth. Wonderful are the words which came from His lips. Wonderful is He in His moral glory, His untiring service, His love, His patience, and everything which the Spirit has been pleased to tell us of His earthly life.

The more our hearts contemplate Him, the more wonderful He appears. But still greater and more wonderful is it that He went to the cross to give His life as a ransom for many, that the Just One should die for the unjust. He is wonderful in His great work on the cross, the depths of which have never been fathomed.

And how wonderfully He has dealt with us, with each one individually. How wonderful is it that He knows each of His sheep, that He guides each, provides for, loves, succors, stands by, restores, never leaves nor forsakes each who belongs to Him. How wonderful is His grace, the supply and fullness of it!

"One evening," said C. H. Spurgeon, "I was riding home after a heavy day's work, weary and sore depressed, when suddenly, as a lightning flash, came: 'My grace is sufficient for thee.' And I said: 'I should think it is, Lord,' and burst out laughing. It seemed to make unbelief so absurd.

"It was as if some little fish, being very thirsty, was troubled about drinking the river dry; and Father Thames said: 'Drink away, little fish, my stream is sufficient for thee.' Or it seemed like a little mouse in the granaries of Egypt after seven years of plenty, fearing it might die of famine, and Joseph might say: 'Cheer up, little mouse, my granaries are sufficient for thee.' Again I imagined a man away up yonder on the mountain saying to himself: 'I fear I shall exhaust all the oxygen in the atmosphere.' But the earth might say: 'Breathe away, O man, and fill thy lungs ever. My atmosphere is sufficient for thee.'"

In His coming manifestation He will be wonderful. Wonderful He will be when we shall see Him and stand in His presence. What a day it will be when we see Him face to face! Then we shall know all the loveliness and wonder of His adorable Person and His wonderful ways with us. With what delight we shall then behold Him!

And when He comes with His saints, when the heavens are lit up with untold glory, when He comes to judge, to establish His kingdom, to speak peace to the nations, to restore creation to its right condition, when He reigns and all His redeemed ones with Him— oh, how wonderful it all will be!

He is altogether lovely, and He is altogether wonderful. Glory to His name! Well has one said:

> He pervades the whole of the New Testament with His presence, so that every doctrine it teaches, every duty it demands, every narrative it records, every comfort it gives, every hope it inspires, gather about His Person and minister to His glory. So dear does He thus become to the heart of the believer, that Luther may well be excused for exclaiming, 'I had rather be in hell with Christ, than in heaven without Him.'

May the Holy Spirit fill our hearts and eyes with Him and reveal to us through the written Word more of the matchless beauty of the wonderful Person of our Saviour and Lord.

Wonder of Wonders

Dawn Finlay

Shall I tell you what I saw?
Camels tethered at the door…
Costly gifts upon the floor…
Kings a-kneeling in the straw,
Lost in wonder, pale with awe,
While a Child smiled!

The Resurrected Christ

W. Graham Scroggie

H ow transcendent a revelation of the power and love of God is the incarnation of His Son! So amazing is His condescension who *"emptied Himself,"* by taking *"the form of a bond-slave,"* by becoming *"in the likeness of men"* and by presenting Himself *"in fashion as a man,"* that thinkers have come to regard this as the whole of the Christian gospel.

But to the incarnation is added the atoning death, that further and deeper humiliation to which the Son of God consented that He might take away the sin of the world (Jn. 1:29). Surely this is the wonder of wonders, and the glory of glories! How can there be anything greater than this?

Yet, this is not the end. Beyond the incarnation and crucifixion, is the resurrection, that stupendous event which called into exercise all *"the strength of God's might"* (Eph. 1:19-20) which surpassed every previous manifestation of the divine power in human history, and to which are attached such momentous issues. And beyond this again, is the exaltation of Jesus to God's right hand; the enthronement in heaven of the Son of Man; the glorification, in the presence of astonished angelic hosts, of Him who was born in a stable.

How sublime a history, and how overwhelming a revelation is this! As we now contemplate it, shall we not ask for the gift of understanding, and the spirit of devotion.

In our thinking we must not leave Christ on the cross; for God did not leave Him there. He *"raised Him from the dead,"* and set Him on the throne, and made Him Lord of all. With what a rebound did the *"energy of the might of God's strength"* put forth itself in Him, when once the great sacrifice was accomplished.

Ephesians 1:20-23 calls attention to three momentous truths, which together constitute the vision of Christ risen and glorified. These are the resurrection of Christ: the life renewed in Him (v. 20a); the exaltation of Christ: the place assigned to Him (v. 20b); and the dominion of Christ: the authority invested in Him (vv. 21-23).

The whole subject emerges from the Apostle's prayer that we might know *"what is the hope of His calling; what the riches of the glory of His inheritance in the saints; and what is the exceeding greatness of His power to usward who believe."* Thus vitally are devotion and doctrine related, and it is only in the spirit of the prayer that we can understand the truth.

"God raised Him from the dead." The historicity of Christ's resurrection is vital for Christianity. Could any of the various theories opposed to the fact be shown to be true, that proof would be the destruction of the Christian's ground of faith and hope. We shall, therefore, view this momentous event in two lights: as an historical fact and as a spiritual truth.

1. THE RESURRECTION AS A HISTORICAL FACT. Alas, that today it should be necessary, as in the first century, to ask, *"Why should it be thought a thing incredible with you, that God should raise the dead?"* (Acts 26:8). Yet necessary it is; for the history of the criticism of the resurrection narratives is one long record of attempts to impugn their trustworthiness and to form hypotheses which are purely naturalistic.

But these numerous attempts notwithstanding, with all the confidence of the first disciples we may affirm our faith in those ringing words, the climax of a great argument, *"But now is Christ risen from the dead, and become the firstfruits of them that slept"* (1 Cor. 15:20).

Christian faith, however, is neither ignorance nor credulity, but rests on a substantial foundation of fact; so that if the resurrection of Christ cannot be shown to be a fact, our faith is at once void and vain (1 Cor. 15:14, 17).

The resurrection of Christ claims to be fact exactly in the same sense as His death and burial claim to be facts, and must be capable of the same kind of proof. Its objectivity is essential to its significance and, brushing aside all mere sophistry, we confidently affirm that if this event be less than fact, it cannot be more than fiction.

It is well, therefore, that we should remind one another of the ground on which our faith rests.

Confining ourselves to the New Testament writings, I would bring to your notice as briefly as possible, some of the evidences on which our belief in the physical resurrection of Christ rests.

Our Lord's being what He was, necessitated it. We can believe in His resurrection if we can believe in Him at all. The event was not more singular and unique than the nature of Him to whom it befell.

If we believe that He was supernaturally born, that He lived without sin, and that He chose to die to bring deliverance to sinners, then not only is it easy to believe that He rose again, but it is impossible to believe that He did not. Not for one moment can we suppose that that holy life, the record of which the Evangelists have given us, should end in its prime in a cruel and shameful death. It is just the holiness of Christ which gives reality and intelligibility to the miracle of His resurrection. Each confirms the other. The sinless man cannot *"be holden of death"*; He must rise again. And He who rose again, never to return to the grave—as did all others who were raised from the dead—must be the sinless man.

With the resurrection of our Lord, everything else that has been revealed of Him assumes proportion, order, and harmony; without it, all is mystery, a lock without a key, a labyrinth without a clue, a beginning without a corresponding end.

The work which Christ came to do required it. To regard the resurrection as merely the reward bestowed on the Son by the Father for His faithfulness unto death is to miss its chief significance. His rising again from the dead was an essential and integral part of the work which He had been sent into the world to accomplish. Speaking of His life He said, *"I have power to lay it down, and I have power to take it again. This commandment received I from My Father"* (Jn. 10:18).

The two parts of this statement must not be separated from one another. The resurrection was as essential a part of the Father's will and of the Son's work as was the crucifixion, and the latter was in order to the former, for He said, *"Therefore do I lay down My life, that I may take it again"* (Jn. 10:17).

When on the Mount of Transfiguration our Lord spoke of the

"exodus" which He should accomplish at Jerusalem, He spoke of more than His death, for *"exodus"* is more than *"decease."* His dying was not a "way out" unless He rose again.

The invariable teaching of the New Testament is that Christ's resurrection was not merely something consequent upon His redemptive work, but an essential part of the work itself. It is the complement of His incarnation, ministration, and crucifixion.

Jesus Himself predicted it. His utterances at first were in vague terms, such as *"Destroy this temple, and in three days I will raise it up."* But later on He spoke plainly, always associating His resurrection with His death. This, then, constitutes an integral part of the claim made for Himself by Jesus Christ, and if He did not rise from the dead, that claim, in all its parts, is invalidated.

But again, the empty tomb demonstrated it. Jesus had died and was buried; yet, after three days, His body had disappeared, and the tomb was empty. What had happened? If His foes had taken His body, then why did they not produce it, to silence forever those who were preaching that the Lord was risen? And if His friends had taken it away, they were not deceived, but deceivers, and the Christian Church was founded and has flourished for nearly nineteen hundred years on a fraud. The fact of the empty tomb stands impregnable against all the attacks of visional and apparitional theories.

The primitive belief is inexplicable without it. Nothing is clearer from the narratives than the utter surprise of the friends of Jesus at His reappearance, and their complete unpreparedness for the event. The words of the two disciples on the way to Emmaus express the condition of mind of all the disciples during the gloomy interval between His death and His resurrection, *"We hoped that it was He who should have redeemed Israel."*

There was no predisposition on their part either to expect that Christ would rise again or to fancy that He had done so. Yet, within six weeks of His death, we find these very men openly declaring that their Master was alive and had been seen by them. The sudden change in these disciples is a fact which demands a full explanation. The removal of the body would not explain it; and three days is not long enough for a legend to spring up which should so affect them. The only explanation is to be found in the fact of the resurrection.

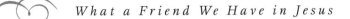

The appearances of our Lord crown the certainty of it. Of these, ten are recorded, within forty days, and probably there were more (Acts 1:3). They were made under a great variety of circumstances; to men and women; to individuals and to groups; in the house and on the street; to disciples joyful and sad. Some of these appearances were momentary, and others were protracted; and in various forms did He manifest Himself to them (Mk. 16:12). It is quite impossible that in all these circumstances, all these people should have been mistaken. The only way to account for this is by the resurrection.

The way in which the event is reported confirms it. It is distinguished by a simplicity which avoids all exaggeration, makes no boast of enthusiastic feeling, and frankly confesses a large measure of ignorance and blindness; whereas, had it been the result of either conscious or unconscious invention, it could hardly have failed to bear marks of the excitement which gave rise to it.

Everywhere in the accounts we observe the indications of reality and personal testimony; everywhere there is the deepest inward evidence of their own literal truthfulness. The Evangelists wrote, not to create belief in the resurrection but to inform those who already believed. Consequently they treat the matter as simply, unaffectedly, and inartificially as everything else which they touch.

The existence of the Christian Church implies it. We cannot think that there could have been a Christian Church at all except for the belief in the resurrection of Christ. The existence of this society is the first and final proof of the historic truth of the miracle on which it was founded. The Church came out of the belief, and the belief came out of the fact of the resurrection.

This is true, not only of the Church herself, but also of her institutions. What was it that occasioned the distinction between the Jewish Sabbath and the Lord's Day, and the sudden change from the one to the other? Only one thing—the belief that Jesus rose from the grave on that first morning of the week.

To all these evidences let us add only one more, namely, the testimony of the Apostle Paul. It is simply incredible that a man of Paul's mentality and education should have come to regard the resurrection of Jesus as absolutely irrefutable, and that, within six years of the supposed event, if in reality it were not a fact. For twenty-five years this man served Christ and suffered for Him as few have done; and the driving conviction behind all was that His Lord was alive and that he had seen Him in the body. The revelation of the risen Christ changed the whole current of his life. It moulded and fashioned him. It filled his life with all that he felt to be worth living for and dying for; and it supplies the key to his system of Christian thought. Such an effect could not be produced but by the fact.

How superabundant then, is the evidence of Christ's resurrection! It is "the best attested fact in history" and "the rock from which all the hammers of criticism have never chipped a single fragment."

2. THE RESURRECTION AS A SPIRITUAL TRUTH. This aspect of it emerges from, and rests on the fact for what is historically false cannot be spiritually true. In the New Testament a heavy superstructure of teaching is built on the declared event. Facts always precede doctrines, and doctrines inevitably grow out of facts. Theology is the child of history, for from the beginning divine revelation was made in human life; so that the Bible is not so much the revelation as the record of it. The resurrection is the revelation of a new life, and, significantly enough, it was made only to disciples. Christ Himself was *"the same,"* for His disciples knew Him; and yet, He was not the same, for "what was natural to Him before is now miraculous, and what was before miraculous is now natural."

Before the cross His spirit was manifested through His body; but after He rose from the grave, His body was manifested by His spirit. He was no longer subject to the laws of the material order to which His earthly life was previously conformed.

Christ in resurrection life is the link between the seen and the unseen. In His resurrection body were blended the earthly and the spiritual, for it had the qualities of the higher sphere to which it belonged, and yet retained the visible marks which demonstrated the identity of the present with the past. The resurrection registers the transition from the historical to the spiritual Christ. Behind Him lay the infancy, the childhood, the manhood, the ministry, the crucifixion and the burial; while before Him there opened the whole length of the life in heaven which, to His humanity, was a new experience.

The resurrection is, therefore, a revelation of the spiritual world, and of our connection with it. This doctrine stands at the very center of the Christian system of truth, and both history and revelation are enigmas without it. It is the event to which all pre-Christian history converged, and from which all Christian history has flowed. It is "at once the end and the beginning of vast developments of life and thought; the climax of a long series of dispensations which find in it their complement and explanation," and we must place it in the very front of our confession, with all that it includes, or we must be prepared to lay aside the Christian name.

The writers of the New Testament have given it a dominating place. The sunlight of the resurrection morning floods all the landscape of the gospel story, in the records of the Evangelists as a fact; in the Book of the Acts as an experience, and in the Epistles as a doctrine. The truth must never be allowed to obscure the fact, nor the fact to take the place of the truth. To preach the fact was the first function of the Evangelists; and to embody the doctrine is the great office of the Church.

The fact of the resurrection, resting on its appropriate evidence, invites us to the consideration of its own transcendental meaning; and this meaning both confirms and glorifies the fact. But it is not enough to believe the fact, and appreciate the truth; we must also know the One who conquered death and now lives in the power of an endless life. The truth of the resurrection ultimately means that, through faith in Him, I have the certain hope of being the eternal companion of the One who said, *"I am He that liveth, and was dead; and, behold, I am alive for evermore, Amen; and have the keys of hell and of death"* (Rev. 1:18).

—*Visions of Christ,* (London: Marshall Bros., 1925), pp. 85-99

An Easter Song

Susan Coolidge

A song of sunshine through the rain,
Of spring across the snow;
A balm to heal the hurts of pain,
A peace surpassing woe.
Lift up your heads, ye sorrowing ones,
And be ye glad at heart,
For Calvary and Easter Day,
Earth's saddest day and gladdest day,
Were just three days apart!

A Friend in Need, a Friend Indeed

J. B. Nicholson, Jr.

We come to the last gilded frame on the picture gallery wall in this collection portraying our Best Friend. I would dare add one last little canvas, selecting for my palate the muted hues of the desert. Desert daylight is harsh and strong, blanching the landscape, bleeding the colors from the sand and sky. The shimmering heat reflecting off the desert floor blurs the details and seems to melt the horizon line. Only in the early morning and at dusk does the scene take on the scarlets and golds of the sun.

Does it often seem that way with our lives? In the early hours of childhood, experiences seem so vivid, life's joys are pure and bright. Even its little sorrows, though sharp, can often be kissed away. And at the other end of life, too, with the encroaching shadows, the things that matter seem to come back into focus. The superficial things—the clothes we wear, the food we eat, our trinkets and toys—seem more willing to loosen their hold on us. As our bodies begin to fail us and temporal hopes recede, we are forced back to simple pleasures, basic needs, and the growing certainty that our limited days should be filled with the things that matter most.

But in the middle years, the harsh realities of human experience seem to bleach the life out of us. The gale-force wind of adversity against us, the battering of emotional storms within us, the increasingly parched world around us, and the glaring searchlight of divine justice above us—these all combine to leave us gasping for something bigger than ourselves. Something secure to give us refuge from the incessantly changing winds. Something to harbor us, a haven where the inner storms somehow cannot reach us. A special kind of water, imported from a Better Land, that will slake our parched souls. And relief from the seemingly merciless rays of divine light that expose us, not for what people think we are, but for what we really are. How far must we search, how many mirages must disappoint us, how many burning steps across the heartless sandscape before we find such a place?

It is the testimony of the world that no such place exists. But, thank the Lord, it is the testimony of God Himself that there is a Person who exactly meets these longings of the wilderness pilgrim.

Among his many canvasses of the Messiah, the inspired word-painter Isaiah describes how it is possible to bring back the color to the wind-swept, storm-battered, desert-parched, sun-beaten soul: *"And a Man shall be as an hiding place from the wind, and a covert from the tempest; as rivers of water in a dry place, as the shadow of a great rock in a weary land"* (Isa. 32:2).

Reading the verse, I can feel the relief flooding in, washing over my spirit. Drink in those blessed words! *An hiding place...a covert... rivers of water...the shadow of a great rock....* This Man of whom Isaiah speaks is absolutely everything we need for the pilgrim journey! There is protection and provision, sustenance and shade. He is the continuing security of a hiding place from the blazing sirocco, interposing Himself between us and its blistering, blinding heat. *"A very present help,"* He provides the ready availability of a covert when out of nowhere an untimely storm catches us, vulnerable and exposed. He slakes our thirst from a river that flows from Himself, our smitten Rock. And when in our weariness—weary perhaps with the hardness of the way, or worse still, the hardness of our own hearts—we drop to our knees in despair, we find the *"Rock that followed them"* through that *"great and terrible wilderness"* is still ready to provide the blessed shadow of Himself as our refuge.

Whatever else we may apply from this portrait of heaven's lovely Man, let us take to our hearts three life-sustaining truths. First, it is obvious that the need is all ours; the provision is all in Him. Second, when feeling my soul is like a desert wasteland, I need to flee *to* Him, not *from* Him. He never yet turned one away, nor ever will. And finally, the journey is often long and hard, but it will surely bring us at last to a land where no storm sweeps its landscape, no weariness plagues its inhabitants. And the Man who traversed the desert with us will meet us on the last mile and bring us safely Home.

What a Man!

H. J. Miles

When the blast's o'erwhelming force
Breaks upon us in its course,
Then a Man shall be, in grace,
From the wind, a hiding-place.

Bursts the tempest, thundering dread,
From the darkening clouds o'erhead,
Sent by God, a Man shall form
Sheltering covert from the storm.

As our eyes in all around
Nothing see but barren ground,
In a Man our hearts shall trace
Rivers in a barren place.

When the sun with scorching ray
Beats upon our pilgrim way,
As a rock a Man shall stand,
Shadow in a weary land.

Jesus! Thou the Hiding-Place,
Covert from the tempest's face,
Waterbrooks where all is dry,
Shading Rock when sun is high.